Body Uptown

Customer Service Fairytales from the Financial Print IPO Market

Laura Melia Kelly

Gatefold Press

Dwayne,
Bourne wouldn't have been the same without you. Thanks for being such a leader xo
fmk

Many thanks to all the folks who assisted with this project and to the friends and early readers who provided invaluable feedback and advice. Thank you.

Cover design:
Jessica Licciardello

Cover photo:
© Stephen O'Byrne
www.sobphotography.net

Gatefold Press logo:
James F. Williams
www.jiminius.com

Printed in the United States of America
First Printing, 2016.
ISBN 978-0-9983890-0-4
Gatefold Press
www.gatefoldpress.com

To all the talented and knowledgeable people around the Financial Print network…

To all the friends who egged me along to complete this compilation with direct or indirect or completely-unknown-to-them encouragement…

To my husband, Gunnar Kelly.

A note from the author…

This is not a tell-all, nor a history of the industry, nor even an accurate representation of anyone else's experience. I only try to capture the essence of the place, the people, my self, as it was to me in that moment in time.

LMK

Body Uptown

Customer Service Fairytales from the
Financial Print IPO Market

Body Uptown —

"Body" is the shorthand used to order a car to carry a passenger, typically a client; used in conjunction with the general direction the car needs to take the passenger (e.g., "body uptown" or "body downtown," as differentiated from "package uptown" or "package downtown")

CORRESPONDENCE

"So, what do you do?"

I hate small talk about work because I work for a financial printer.

"Oh, a financial printer…," my cocktail companion will say, trailing off as they realize they have no idea what that means.

Financial print is an industry within the financial markets. We work with attorneys, investment bankers, and issuers to get documents drafted, filed with the Securities and Exchange Commission (the "SEC"), printed, and distributed to the street. It's a 24-hour, male-dominated, deadline-driven business.

"Ohhh… so you, print money?" say six out of the ten victims. The other four just nod and pretend they understand. It's okay, we can move on. But they don't know what they're missing.

No.

No money. Not money how you think of it anyway.

"You know the mutual fund prospectus you get every once in a while from your 401-K that you open, pretend to look at, and then throw in the trash?" I like to say. Sudden nods of recognition. "That's us."

But we also typeset, file, and/or print Initial Public Offerings (IPOs), Annual Reports, current report filings (8-Ks), bankruptcy and merger documents, and a slew of other financial books and materials that drive corporate finance activity. The SEC has hundreds of required filing form types.

The problem with my mutual fund answer is two-fold: (1) I work in capital markets not mutual funds, although of course mutual funds are part of our business. But most financial printers have a definitive separation between capital markets and mutual funds, because the requirements are so different. Mutual funds? Those guys could have 24-48 hours to turn stuff around—it's all planned out with a grid of the fund's entire yearly cycle. They know exactly what they're getting, when they're getting it, and where it has to go—which is precisely the opposite of how financial print works in capital markets. And, so, thus, (2) My layman's explanation does a piss-poor job of explaining what being a New York Financial Print Customer Service Rep is really all about. And that's a shame, because what we do is pretty kickass amazing. It's also stressful, life-consuming, and at times fairly miserable because you basically want to kill everybody every moment of your day for about 90% of the time you spend as a rep in Customer Service. And that's on the good days.

Financial print is not like publishing or even commercial print. It's a whole other animal. The documents are strictly confidential. Deadlines and turnarounds are extremely tight. The slowest typesetting turnaround in financial print is "Overnight." The fastest is just minutes. Edit rounds (which are clients' markup or what we call "AA's" for "Author's Alterations") are constant. Clients can make changes to their document up until literally moments before the SEC's daily filing deadline. Every second counts. Certain reports are created, typeset, and filed with the government all on the same day, sometimes in an hour or two. Other deals could extend for months, as clients get comments from the SEC, make revisions, and execute amendment filings and ultimately multiple printings. The margin for error is virtually zip, with errors or non-compliance potentially resulting in millions of dollars in fines or losses. A print run turnaround for thousands of copies is typically 12 or 16 hours, not days or weeks as in other print sectors. Requirements for delivery are strict and production can include timely submissions to markets and regulators across the globe. Need to put a man on the Concorde to get it there on time? Done. It's not even a question.

During the IPO Market of the late 1990s, a New York Financial Print Customer Service Rep could easily work at least a dozen deals like this at once, and regularly into two or three dozen. And then there are the hours. Come in four hours early? Hang four hours late? Maybe eight hours late? Saturday? Sunday? We're open 24 hours a day, you see, 365 days a year. Alright, we're closed on Christmas. Unless a client wants to come in. Then we're open.

So when I'd try to explain how busy it is when we're busy and someone's like, "Oh, yeah, it gets really busy at my job, I know."

No.

You really don't know.

In those days, a hundred miles an hour with your hair on fire was a good starting point. Then light everything around you on fire as well. And then cue the screams. Feel like killing anyone yet?

But it was also more nuanced than that.

Someone once described financial print to me as "blue-collar workers in a white-collar world." We were white-collar and we catered to Wall Street, but we weren't in that echelon. Sure, we wore the best suits we could afford and got bonuses in the good years and even had a few enviable perks like tickets to the box at Madison Square Garden or however-brief interactions with the famous names that grace the world's biggest companies…

But we weren't Wall Street.

We weren't bankers.

We weren't lawyers.

We were printers.

We had our own language, our own shorthand. I will not bore you here with explanations or definitions of financial print jargon, but there's a glossary at the back of this book that I hope will cover anything you get stuck on. Also, we cursed a lot, so if that isn't for you, you should stop reading now and give this book to an attorney or banker to enjoy.

For me the most fun years in financial print were spent in Customer Service. We were a perfect storm of a department, growing rapidly in a hot market and perpetually on the verge of lunacy. The job has changed a lot since my time in the 1990s. Some clients have brought their document preparation and filing activity into their own operations; they no longer need a financial printer to do as much of the process for them. Advancements in word processing and electronic delivery have squeezed out the need for the craftsmanship of typeset print production and for the fire drill of Customer Service Reps running through airports with rush roadshow deliveries. Different output formats and government regulations are now in effect.

Office work in the '90s now seems as antiquated as we thought the '50s were then. We had computers, of course—our typesetting interface a DOS-like affair and our blue-screened email system with yellow type—but for all purposes ours was still a paper-based world. To send a client's Word (or WordPerfect!) file to another site meant putting their 3.5-inch disk into a shoebox-sized machine called a diskfax and dialing a number to transmit it. And then hoping it went through—you could never really be sure until you called to follow up. Sending a proof to a country where we had affiliates instead of offices involved computerized transmittal over phone lines, a process that could take upwards of an hour and had to be re-started if the affiliate's machine ran out of paper or jammed or had chickens standing on it (yes, this actually happened once) or was unplugged at four o'clock in the morning. It's nice those things are in the past.

But I think the most drastic and soul-killing change is that clients don't need to come to the financial printer's office to work their deals anymore. Not with the numbers or purpose they once did. Before email and PDFs were ubiquitous, Customer Service was a physical madhouse with dozens of clients working in our New York City offices around the clock. It was loud. It was movement. Phones ringing non-stop. Banks of beeping fax machines and Xeroxes churning and print devices screeching out their pages. People shouting and running. Clients everywhere: in the hallways, the conference rooms, at the counter. They paid our bills and got their deals done. We worked their pages and printed their jobs. We basically did whatever they asked us to. We made it happen.

It's quiet now. Comparatively, anyway. I've been off the floor a long time but it seems to me there's a lot of typing and not as much talking. Markup arrives silently, electronically, instead of by sweaty messenger or slanted fax. And clients email instead of call, even for the all-important "OK to File."

Our tangible artifacts—all the paper we kept with the "job bag" (the physical file of a deal), the proofs and work orders and client memos and as-filed masters—are gone. You don't need to run out hard copies of the document like you used to. You don't photocopy changed pages to send ten simultaneous faxes to ten different working group members. It still exists of course, in the computer. Just not exactly with you. Maybe not as much yours.

In the paper-based world you could tell how big or complicated a deal was by the job bag. An 8-K, typically a same-day three-page document, had a thin slim bag, only housing two or three short work orders (the official instructions CS issues to record activity on the deal), the tiny proof (a copy of the document), a couple of fax distributions and an SEC acceptance before it left Customer Service to be passed through to the Pricing Department for invoicing. A tender offer or IPO would have our same standard oak tag bag, only its would be stretched out from 160-page proofs being jammed into it and pulled out of it shift after shift. Bags ragtag from being pushed around people's desks and thrown on counters over weeks or months. These bags were veterans—notes and numbers graffitied on their outsides, instructions stapled to their fronts, Pantone chips taped to them for reference. Deals growing to multiple bags to hold exhibits or disks or packs of labels for the print distribution. Rubber bands strained around them to keep the sides from splitting out from so much content. Ah, the job bags. At many printers even the job bag itself is now a thing of the past. It's all in the computer. It wasn't that long ago, was it?

But I digress. Listen to me go on about job bags! What I mean to say is this book isn't about Wall Street or about the financial markets. It's not about job bags.

My old company no longer exists and neither does the New York of that time. New York will never have the same energy as those pre-9/11 years. The new New York meets you for a drink and is perfectly capable of having a grand memorable time, but the old New York is the charismatic arrogant balls-out personality who's open-mouth laughing with you as he slams his drink on the bar at 3AM and then appears across the desk from you four hours later to work his ass off. And he does it all again tomorrow.

He's 25, after all.

And so I suppose this compilation is an exercise in nostalgia.

We were young.

We were reps.

On our best days we worked hard, we played hard, we had a lot of laughs. In many ways we were like a crazy dysfunctional family.

In our darker moments we were irreverent, often politically incorrect. We were adrenalin-fueled junkies bubbling over with stress, lashing out at those in our path one second and then assuming a submissive gorilla posture in the conference room as a client tore us a new one in the next. We felt the resigned defeat of a job gone wrong that can't be fixed, the unbridled anger that slams your phone receiver on the desk until it breaks, the offense of billing out your annual salary in a day while the salesman bounds out for dinner, and the frustration of the middle child, caught between the actions of other departments or shifts, left to find a way to put a good spin on it for the client and, in lieu of that, to be the punching bag.

"It is what it is," we'd say to each other. "You're gonna have to suck it up."

And so we did.

But when things went right, which they also did, plenty of times, you felt like gold, diamonds even, like true heroes. Pulling a win from the depths of potential tragedy we'd hail: "YES! How fucking good am I?" Moving our job bags around with Cheshire smiles, sometimes we could all feel that victory. "You're fucking good," we'd say back. "Fucking amazing."

7

Sometimes I wonder what the effects are on the human body of feeling such a range of emotions at a pace so accelerated, to do it over and over again day after day and year after year. Some reps quit. Some snap. Some drink or party. Many continue on or move on, but take years to recover. Some just stop caring. In those days there were not many reps over the age of 40. Almost all of New York Customer Service's second and third shift were under 30 years old.

And yet, woven through the anger and the stress and the highs and the lows and the unending breakneck speed, there were moments. Moments of connection, of laughter, of absurdity, of sublime execution. Bits that were a spot of humanity translatable to any industry, maybe, to an age, a feeling. That's what this book is about, perhaps. The things that stayed with me, that were meaningful to me. It is not comprehensive, nor meant to be. It's simply what stuck.

Here are some of my favorite (publishable) memories from those days.

PART I

Fordham

"Well, your resume looks in order," the middle-aged woman at Fordham's career center told me. Her fingers played down the text containing the three jobs and ten or twelve accompanying bullets that summarized the last (and only) five years of my work experience. "You've got a strong work history…"

"I'm getting a lotta interviews but no call backs."

"You're an English major?"

"Yeah, I was doubling with Elementary Ed but I dropped the Ed in the fall."

"I see," she said. "And I see you've gone to our interview workshop… You did well, so that's not the problem…"

I'd immersed myself in job search materials my senior year in college. I knew my interview questions backwards and forwards, I was confident. I had examples from my work history, evidence of being promoted. I was ready. In the fall, I'd gotten called for five interviews, I thought they went well—all New York City jobs, entry-level, accepting liberal arts majors. But no callbacks. It was spring now, just a few months to graduation, and I needed to land a job. Anywhere. Any job. I had rent to pay and time was running out. I wanted a good-sized company, somewhere I could get in and hopefully move up. I'd come to the career center to figure out my problem. Why was I getting interviews but no call backs? What was I doing wrong?

She looked at me. Looked in my eyes, but then looked at the rest of me. I was slim, casually dressed in jeans and a flannel; it was the '90s. My long brown hair, kind of an untamable curly, falling down to my elbows. She looked down at my resume. Back at me.

"It's your hair," she concluded, setting my paper on her counter.

I stared at her.

"Really?" I said.

"Don't take this the wrong way…," she said, "but you wanna look like someone's employee, not like someone's date."

I stood there. Change my hair? Is she serious? She could tell I was skeptical.

"Cut your hair, hon. Shoulder length, tops. See what happens. You can always grow it back."

She handed my resume back to me, her work complete.

I went home. A month went by, as I applied for the next round of job openings advertised through the career center. I got a haircut. Got called for three more interviews.

And got three offers.

It was totally the hair.

Day 1

I followed him through the department, winding around counters and desks and other employees walking with missions I did not yet understand.

"You have a passport?" he called over his shoulder.

"No," I said.

My parents were schoolteachers from Brooklyn; I came from a family of driving vacations. With the exception of a monumentally torturous family trek across the western US in the '80s and a trip to Florida's Disney World in the earlier '80s, I'd barely been off the east coast, let alone out of the country.

"Get a passport. And keep it on you. You never know when they're gonna need someone to fly."

"Okay."

He shook someone's hand and patted another guy on the back as we turned through another set of desks. This company occupies five floors of a building the size of a city block and Customer Service and its peripheral departments consume an entire floor. It's a maze of hallways and doors and short-walled cubicles and ramps, with stairwells that only go up and others that only go down. I tried to remind myself it was like freshman year—that the floor plan seemed confusing but I'd figure it out fast enough.

"Where'd you go to school?" he said as we arrived at a clearing.

"Fordham."

"Alright then, Fordham," he said looking around. "Let's see, who else went to Fordham?" he said to himself. "See that woman over there? The one in blue?" I recognize Terri Hansen from my interview and am grateful. "Her name's Terri, go sit by her. Tell her you're her new rep."

"Okay, thanks," I said. I headed off toward Terri to start my first day as a New York Customer Service Rep. At that moment I had no idea what the job I'd accepted even was.

When in Doubt

"I tell all the new reps: There's only three rules in Customer Service," the salesman said, stretching his arms across the counter and placing his palms flat on either side of the document master.

"If you don't know... ask."

Alright, I nodded.

"When in doubt... call."

Okay, sounds reasonable.

"And..."

He retracted and brushed his hair back with his hand.

"Don't get offended."

It Was the Best of Times...

It was 1996 and we were running.

Deals were falling out of the sky, half of them IPOs. We didn't know it yet but within a year our department would practically double in size, the company hiring New York Customer Service Reps in droves as new reps who couldn't hack the hours or the stress dropped out every month.

Clients were in our offices around the clock. They came for drafting sessions, for the OK to File, for the OK to Print. They came to clear an SEC package, to look at colorwork, to review a bookproof. They came any hour and would stay for any length of time. Some stayed for days—eating, sleeping, and showering in our offices.

In the end, they came to turn pages. They'd mark up more pages or have a drink and eat while their pages turned. They'd look at the boats on the Hudson River, maybe shoot a game of pool in the lounge to pass the time. In the evenings, they might retreat to a darkened TV room for a smoke or to catch the score on the ballgame.

Once I found a client giving another client a tour. "He's never been to the printer before," he said to me while his colleague gaped at our arcade-sized video games and the filet mignon and lobster tail buffet.

One night I spied my heavyset client standing by the floor-to-ceiling windows in the lounge as the dark descended. One hand in his suit pocket, tie loosened from thirty-six hours of wear, he watched the lights of New Jersey appear as he chomped his cigar. This is New York, I thought, and we're in it.

But first, the pages.

We had typesetting sites all over the country, but these were the days before a true Composition Platform. You had to shop your jobs around, calling out to all sites, splitting jobs up as needed to make the turnarounds your clients wanted, which was generally as soon as possible or first thing in the morning.

These were also the days before PDF distributions, so Customer Service had to account for complete logistics, making sure to get jobs back with enough time to Xerox and messenger proofs to whatever locations they needed to be.

We were on the edge of a technological revolution. The SEC had recently begun accepting filings electronically for domestic issuers. Clients had just started using email. Our manufacturing plant had been moved out of Manhattan to New Jersey, and the typesetters in New York were dwindling.

But we weren't there yet. Most every client still sent their markup in via fax or messenger, conversions came in by floppy disk, we had typists and support people and runners. We had a row of chairs in Shipping where flannel-clad messengers awaited the next rush package to run out of the building. A hallway of suited drivers loitering for the next rush drop to Connecticut or Westchester.

We were one foot in and one foot out. We were making money. And we were busy.

A cross between an emergency room and a trading floor, New York Customer Service was so busy you literally did not have time to go to the bathroom. Reps would hold their pee for hours. So busy you would not get a drink of water for fear that the ten-second walk to the water cooler would set you so far behind that, after a quick calculation of the current priorities, it was preferable to die of thirst. That kind of busy.

The times were mayhem.

But oh, the pages. How we all needed the fucking pages.

New York Customer Service

BzzzBING! Time stops as everyone looks to the board to see which conference room is ringing. 21. We're still looking at it when bzzzBING! 16 appears.

Ring, ring. "New York Customer Service," someone answers. "Okay, yes, one moment."

"Joe, you've got Toronto on 8-0."

Ring, ring. "New York Customer Service."

We're packed tonight. Every conference room full, some groups stacked up in makeshift areas in the lounge or hallway alcoves instead of a proper room. One group is in a sales office on the floor below us.

A guy from Shipping appears. "Miss Laura, package from Milbank," he hands me the Redweld. "Thanks," I say and open it. Jeez, another convert new for the morning.

"Laura, Phoenix needs you to re-fax cornermark 90 on Multi-canal."

"The English or the Spanish?" I say.

He shrugs his shoulders. Great. Don't take my phone calls,

dude.

BzzzBING! We all look at the board. 5. If you've ever doubted the veracity of Pavlov's dog experiments, spend an afternoon in New York Customer Service and witness a room of homo sapiens react to the in-house buzzer.

I speed dial Phoenix. "Yeah, this is Laura in New York. Someone just called looking for cornermark 90 of the Multicanal inhouse. Do you need the English or the Spanish?"

Ring.

"New York Customer Service."

"Dawn!! Jose from Goldman Prospectus Department coming at you on 5-0!"

More pages are coming out of the printer. Our typesetting sites output completed pages back to us as they're finished. Each team has four industrial printers spitting out pages and three fax machines to send rush outgoing. All incoming faxes go to the fax room.

I scrawl out "CM 90 Multicanal English" with the job number on a fax coversheet and dial the BPX In-House fax from memory. Green button. SEND. I make my rounds to the printers looking for pages of my jobs.

BzzzBING! 19.

Ring, ring. "New York Customer Service."

I'm matching up my fresh pages from the printer to my client's markup: PN 003, PN 045, PN 100, PN 102.

BzzzBING! 14.

Ring. "New York Customer Service."

"Jesus Christ, people," I say to no one. PN 133, PN 134, PN 137.

I make a copy of my fresh pages. Bring changed pages to my conference room. Hurry back again through the dimmed green hallway that laps our floor, a U-shaped highway of conference rooms that hog all the views to the outside world. A client lounge runs the length of the side of the building facing the water and CS is the interior within the square, split by a set of elevators and stairwells. We have open-air pass-throughs on either side of the department—two wide counters clients can walk up to, and an array of doors spaced 20 feet apart so CS can go in and out for fastest access to the conference rooms from anywhere in the department. When I click-swish the door to Customer Service open, the peaceful seal of hallway waters is broken and the sound of overlapping voices, Xerox machines, Bates stampers, phones ringing, and paper rustling washes over me.

Ring. Ring.

"New York Customer Service," I answer at my desk. It's Dallas.

"Laur, you got Lee at BBC on 8-5." I acknowledge and put Dallas on hold.

"Edwin, you got Dallas on 8-2," I say.

"Joe, Traffic says your proofs are up on Project Orange," someone says. Mergers and takeovers work under project names selected by the working group, with varying results: Project Moxie, Project Winnebago, Project Lion King.

The Production Manager appears. "Laura, here's your bookproof on Teletras."

"Thanks, Mitch."

"Got anything for the shuttle?" he says to the team. We've got a van that runs back and forth between Manhattan and our manufacturing plant in Secaucus 24 hours a day. What's that job like, I wonder, just driving back and forth through the Holland Tunnel all day and all night?

"I'm good," I say.

"Me too."

I pick up Lee. "This is Laura," I say into the phone.

"Hold on, Mitch, I've got some labels."

BzzzBING! 7.

"Is Republic of Turkey a self or separate cover?" someone calls out.

"Separate! Do they have my timing yet?" another shouts back from the counter where she's matching up pages.

A runner from the fax room careens around our bank of desks and counters. "Fax from Cravath? Something about Bolivia?" I wave my hand wildly, phone in my ear.

"Turkey is separate, do you have the timing?" A pause. "What's the run?" he calls back.

BzzzBING! We look up. 16 again.

"15,000!"

"IS SOMEONE WORKING AN IN-HOUSE FOR SAN DIEGO??" a rep in the distance shouts.

"15,000," he relays.

"No, Lee, it's the map on Cover 2 they're talking about," I say into the phone.

BzzzBING! Eyes to the board. 1.

"16 hours on Turkey!"

Ring, ring. "New York Customer Service." A pause. "Okay, cool, thanks a lot."

"Atlanta is open for conversions if you got anything!" the rep announces to the room.

I hang up with Lee and am all over that. Speed dial Atlanta 103-20 as I flip through the Milbank package to see how many pages it is.

"Typesetting, please." I skim the client's distribution instructions to see what city's gonna need proofs the earliest. All east coast drops. I ruffle the fax from Cravath and glance over their instructions: New York, New York, South America, Miami, shit, one in London for the morning.

"Team B, I'm transferring Wachtell over to you!" someone shouts.

"Hey, it's Laura in New York, I hear you're open for conversions?... Haha yeah news travels fast here, dude, it's New York... I got about 80 pages text for 6AM." A pause. "Yeah, I can get it to you in the next 15 minutes. Hey, I got 20 pages AA's on another job for 3AM, can you take that too?"

Ring, ring, "New York Customer Service."

"Joe, Maureen in Phoenix on 8-0."

"Thanks," I say, telling Atlanta the job names and numbers. "Thanks." I hang up.

Joe picks up the phone and walks away from the desk, his 20-foot phone cord wrapping around him. "Maureen, honey, where are my pages? I'm growin' old over here..."

I bump up my jobs and write work orders for Atlanta.

BzzzBING! 10.

Ring, ring. "New York Customer Service."

BzzzBING! 12.

That's me. I rush to the conference room, hustle back with more pages past the other teams in CS. The room is on fire.

"Goddamn it!" someone yells from the Xerox machine by Team A. "Why doesn't anyone refill the goddamn copy machine when you see it's running low?!" The sounds of industrial-sized copy machine doors and drawers slamming open and shut. A ream of paper being smashed open on the edge of a counter.

BzzzBING! I look over my shoulder at the in-house board as I'm walking. 3. BzzzBING! Look again. 21. Walking, walking. BzzzBING! One more time. 16.

Man, I feel bad for whoever's got 16, that room will not fucking stop.

Two post-its are on my terminal by the time I get back to my desk.

Ring. Ring, ring. "Joe, you got Judy on 8-0."

Bump my in-house pages, copy my in-house pages, stuff them on the fax machine to Phoenix typesetting.

I dial Shipping and tuck the phone into my neck. I'm marking the red herring on my bookproof so the client can see the color break while I wait for Shipping to pick up. "Red 185," I tag in pencil. Shipping answers.

"Hey, Kenny, it's Laura, listen, I need three cars," I say at a mile a minute.

"Hello, sweetheart," he says in a slow, calm voice, knowing full well that we are fuck-slammed busy. "How you doin' tonight?"

"Oh, no, Kenny, how are YOU doing?" I say, changing my tone to completely relaxed. "We're just kicking back over here, you know, enjoying the sunshine, I'm brushing up on my needlepoint. How's the family?"

"You're crazy, girl," he says, laughing.

"You have no idea," I say, back at a New York pace. "So listen, three cars. One package downtown on 24536, one package Connecticut on 23997, and one body uptown on Room 12. I'm coming over with the packages and'll pick the voucher."

"You got it, three cars, two package, one body."

I press the phone's plunger down and release it to dial again. I return my first post-it, the client call.

Ring. "New York Customer Service."

"Rob, you've got Armando on 8-1."

Then return the call from Cleveland.

Print out my work orders for Atlanta. Stuff those onto another fax machine with their pages. Stick the floppy disk into the diskfax to transfer the file.

"Melia, Judy wants to talk to you next," Joe says. "She's on 8-0."

"Laura, Tom Greyson from Willkie Farr on 8-5."

"Okay."

More pages are coming out of the printer. This night was insane.

I pick up the client, he tells me he's OK to File.

Then Judy. "Yeah," I say, "They're OK to File... Okay... I'm on my way over there, I'll let you know."

Ring, ring. "New York Customer Service," Joe answers. A pause. "Yeah, okay, bring it over here."

"Team A's got a proof distro in Australia. Edwin, you take it. Dwayne's gonna bring it over here," Joe says, as he adjusts the job number on his Bates stamper, turning the cylinder of numbers with the tip of his pen.

BzzzBING! I look to the board. Not me.

I grab my labels, greensheets, and my bookproof and start over to Shipping. Fast, furious footsteps, baby. I stop at the EDGAR room and step in. EDGAR is the acronym for the SEC's system for receiving submissions.

"The Satellite S-3," I announce, and wait for someone to acknowledge my presence. He does. "Is OK to File," I complete my sentence.

Our EDGAR guy looks to the dozens of post-its taped to his overhead counter, slips his finger under one and consciously peels it off. "Satellite S-3," he says, "Got it."

How they keep track of all these filings is truly amazing.

I step back into the thoroughfare toward Shipping. Say drive-by hellos as a rep and then a salesman fly past me in the opposite direction. At the shipping counter I see Kenny. Slap my distros down on his counter.

"Long time, no see, baby. The bookproof's for the Connecticut. I'll be right back with the other."

I turn out and head to Xerox. Find my as-filed on the Xerox proofs counter, check them quickly, and pull a box of blue tape from under the binding counter.

BzzzBING! I look up at the display hanging in the Xerox Department. 16. Jesus. What is your problem, 16??

I jump onto an open binding machine. A support person from Team B is beside me binding an entire cart of someone's job. Luckily, I only have two books to do. The heartbeats of three huge Xerox machines are beating over each other behind me da-dum-da-dum-da-dum-da-dum as I slide the tape in for book #1. It starts to heat-set.

"Laura Melia, please call 7-2-8-0," the overhead announces over the din, "Laura Melia. 7-2," a pause for effect, "8-0."

I pick up the phone on the wall by the binding machine and dial.

"Melia?" Joe answers.

"What's up."

"I've got Tom Greyson from Willkie, says it's an emergency."

"7-4-3-0," I say to communicate my location. I press the receiver's button down with my finger and wait for the phone to ring. RING.

"Laura Melia," I say as I pull book #1 out of the machine. "Hi, Tom… Yes… Okay, hold on, let me see if I can stop it."

I press hold. Dial EDGAR.

"EDGAR Department."

"It's Laura. Satellite S-3 just busted a page, did you file it yet?"

"HOLD THE SATELLITE S-3!" I hear him shout to his

room through a muffled receiver. "Did it file?" he says to someone. "Okay, you're good," he says back to me.

"Not filed?"

"Not filed."

"Thanks," I hang up and pick up Tom.

"Tom, it hasn't filed, we're holding it... Yes, okay, just one page?" I check the clock, they're cutting it close. "Fax it now, okay?"

I hang up and shuffle book #2 into the binding machine. Slip tape #2 into the machine's side. Heat-set, god, five seconds is an eternity. Done. The tape is still hot as I head back to Shipping.

"Oh baby, we're runnin' tonight!" I shout to Kenny as I speed-walk back into Shipping. Nights like these you're on full adrenalin.

He smiles, hanging up his phone from another call. "Always, baby, we're always runnin'!"

"Here's the as-filed for the package downtown," I put the taped books on his counter.

"And here's your voucher for Room 12," he says.

"Love doin' business with ya, Ken," I give him a wink as I turn away.

"Keep runnin', sweetheart! The night is young!"

I head up a ramp into the adjoining fax room.

"Hey, Charlie, I'm looking for a one-page from Willkie, can you let me know as soon as it comes through?"

BzzzBING! I look out his door to the board. 9.

"Of course, my dear," he says. "Oh wait," he says as one of the fax machines comes to life. "This is it!"

"Thanks," I take the page and its cover from him.

I head back to the other side of the building toward Room 12 with the voucher for my in-house client and my one-page emergency fax to be processed.

I drop off my client's voucher and return to my desk. I bump my one-page emergency, copy it, fax it to the typesetting site, and then call them to make sure they know it's psycho-rush for a filing. No such thing as too much follow up; that's how I was taught.

I'm standing at my counter patching my master for Room 12 when another rep rushes over to the fax machine near me, hands full of pages.

Ring. "New York Customer Service," someone answers behind us.

"You know we're totally on TV in some other country," he says, bent over and stuffing pages onto the fax machine.

"Ha," I say, licking my finger and pulling another page out of my master. I turn it facedown on my garbage pile and slip its replacement into the place I'm holding open. Flick through the corner of the proof to find the location of the next page I need to patch.

"It's called Customer Service: *Nights*," he jokes, referencing the Baywatch spinoff.

I laugh. Honestly, if it wasn't for the laughing, we'd probably all be dead.

BzzzBING! We look up at the board.

16, fucking 16 again.

The Players

A New Rep's Guide to Your In-House Clients:

THE ATTORNEYS

Your first introduction is to the main attorney. He's the most senior attorney on this deal under the partner. He's been working 18 hours a day for the last five years. You know this guy, you've already been dealing with him for weeks. You probably also know at least one of his underlings.

Your main attorney is in charge of drafting the document, collecting changes from the rest of the working group, resolving conflicting changes, and submitting edits to the printer. He'll tell you how to conduct the proof distributions—the drafts of revisions sent to the rest of the working group. There will be two or three attorneys from the main firm on a typical job. If it's a big job, or a high-profile job, there will be more. Other law firms will be involved depending how many companies and banks are involved in the deal. Each will have their own law firm and their own set of attorneys making requests, but all the changes to the document will go through the main. The main attorney will set the tone for the whole transaction. You can make a guess about which way it's gonna go by what firm they're from; there's a cultural component to every law firm.

In the conference room, these guys are huddled together marking stuff up. Look for the messiest part of the table and those are the attorneys. All the pages go through them.

THE BANKERS

These guys are underwriting the deal. They'll take a look at things once the attorneys do all the heavy lifting. All they really care about is the front and back cover, where their names appear. They won't even show up for a regular drafting session. The lead underwriter will check that the book's style reflects their bank and will put the prices in at the end. The lead decides how many books are going to be printed, what the deadlines are, and how to distribute the print run.

Look at the cover of your deal. Whoever's name is biggest is the lead. They have thirty deals on their mind and the deal you are working on is merely a distraction from the other twenty-nine. Don't be offended. You can usually find this guy in the hallway on his phone.

THE ACCOUNTANTS

The numbers bunch, these folks are looking at specific pages in the financials. They are efficient. They know their task, they get it done, they'll never ask you for anything. They're in the corner gorging themselves on Volare's and other food they never get to eat unless they're in-house. Pay no attention to these people.

THE COMPANY

This is the issuer everyone is working the deal for. If the deal's an IPO, this is the most exciting time of their lives. If it's a merger, it's the most stressful period they've had this year. If it's a compliance document, it's their normal course of business. It doesn't matter, be nice to everyone from the issuer. They pay the bill.

HONORABLE MENTION: THE PROOFREADERS

These folks come with the attorneys if the job is big enough. They'll be there all night, may take their shoes off and walk around your office, and will always be hungry. You will know who these people are because they'll be the only ones not wearing suits. Depending how un-tucked they are, they may be given their own small conference room near the main room. When they finally leave, you will order them a car going to Queens or Brooklyn.

On the IPO Market

The dayside Production Manager has a page of the *Wall Street Journal* pinned up in his cube. It's a photo of a banker with Alan Greenspan's face tattooed on his bicep.

Return to Sender

"I'm sorry, you say your book is missing what page?" I say into the phone.

"It's more than a page, it jumps from 28 to 51!" the client responds.

Oh fuck, that means the bindery must have missed a form.

"Is it all the copies or just one?"

"No, some are fine, but, hold on…"

I start scratching out a pickup slip while I'm waiting.

"Oh my god, this one is missing pages from the Financial Highlights!"

Fuck. The Financial Highlights are further back in the book. Who knows what happened. Goddamn Monday mornings. This is the thing about working dayside: all the bullshit. On nights you're just a workhorse, processing, processing, processing, clearing jobs to file and print, rushing things out for the FedEx deadline, getting things done. Days is all about 'Oh, my books are fucked up' and 'Do you have a copy of the filing we did three months ago?' People coming up from Pricing asking questions about work orders written six weeks before, salesmen looking for samples of obscure paper stocks. Nights thinks dayside does nothing all day, hell, that's what I thought when I was on nights. But the truth is we're just chasing around bullshit. And third shift —the lobster shift, as we call it—well, that's all about clean up and getting morning proofs out. This dayside gig is just a stint for me, I'm filling in while someone's on maternity leave.

"Sir, I'm so sorry, I'm gonna have a messenger come pick those books up from you right now so we can see what's going on."

"I'm gonna call the attorneys and see if their books are good."

"Alright, I'll call you back once we see the books and know what happened."

An hour later the messenger returned with the client's box of books. Something definitely went wrong in the bindery when this thing went through, almost every book was missing a form, but no consistency on which form was missed.

Within the hour a few other boxes had been returned; clients just started sending bad books back to us, I suppose on the instruction of the guy from the company.

By noon, my desk had become a fort, piled with boxes and envelopes of bad books coming back from attorneys, accountants, and every underwriter on the deal. There were boxes stacked four feet high on my counter, piles behind my chair —the freaking things were everywhere, and they wouldn't stop coming. One client must have thrown out their original packaging; she sent 175 books back in open shopping bags from Lord & Taylor. It was actually becoming comical if you could get over the utter misery of it.

"What's this?" the sales coordinator says when she arrives for her mid-day rounds.

"Job got screwed up in the bindery and now the clients are sending bad books back to us," I say from behind my shelter.

"Oh my god," she says, flipping through a sample, as another messenger arrives with two more boxes. "What was the run?"

I stand up and meet her eyes over a top box.

"Seven thousand."

She cracks a grimaced smile.

"Aaaand…," she says, surveying the stacks, "they're ALL coming back?"

"It appears that way," I report.

We burst into laughter.

We have to laugh or else we'd cry.

Hammer & Nail

"Hey, Laura, could you watch my in-house?"

"Nope." I focused on my computer screen. Everyone knows nothing good comes from watching someone else's in-house.

"Come on… I wanna run down for an egg sandwich."

"Shoulda thoughta that this morning." Unfamiliar document, unfamiliar clients, unknown history, and you can bet as soon as the rep leaves, those clients will ring the bell asking for something.

"Pleeeeease? They're so quiet. It's just one guy in there. I'll bring you back something…" It was 8:30 in the morning, generally a slow time for in-house activity, hardly anyone clears to file or print so early.

I rolled my eyes at Nick but he could see I was folding.

"Fifteen minutes, max, swear."

"Alright, alright."

"He's in 3, AA's at BPX but he hasn't turned a page yet," he said as he headed for the door.

About forty seconds passed before the inevitable.

BzzzBING!

"Three, up on the board!!" the manager shouted.

A red three appeared on our racetrack-style display hanging high on the wall of the department. Conference Room 3, the in-house I was now responsible for, had rung for their Customer Service rep, who was now me.

"Great," I said to my colleague at the next desk. I headed down to Conference Room 3.

I opened the door and saw the lone client.

"Where's Nick?" he wanted to know.

"He had to step away for a few minutes, can I help you with something?"

"Well, yes…," the client started.

I waited. He seemed unsure.

"Do you have a hammer?" he asked.

"Excuse me?"

"A hammer," he said.

"Like a hammer, the tool?"

"Yes, can you get me one?"

This was a question I had never encountered.

"Do you mind if I ask what it's for?" I said.

"You see, there's a lot of construction going on outside…" It was true, the front of our building was surrounded in scaffolding. "And I must have stepped on something, well, a nail apparently…" He lifted up his foot. Yes, there seemed to be a nail sticking out of the side of his shoe. "And now when I cross my legs…" He made his legs into the shape of the number four, lifting his ankle to his opposite knee. "Well, as you can see, it's wearing a hole in the leg of my suit."

A quandary indeed.

"I need to get this nail out," he finished.

"Let me see what I can do, okay?"

Jesus Christ, I needed more coffee.

"Thank you."

I headed back to my desk.

"The freaking guy wants a hammer to pull a nail out of his shoe," I said to the girl at the next desk.

"What??"

"I'm not kidding."

"Call Maintenance," she said. Good idea.

I dialed Maintenance.

"Hey, Brian, it's Laura in Customer Service. Can I borrow a hammer for about 15 minutes for an in-house?"

"Okay. But, uh… why?"

"We've got a client with a nail in his shoe, and—don't ask." He laughed.

"I'll be right over."

"Nick is never gonna believe this," the girl next to me said.

I returned to the conference room with the hammer. It was a strange feeling going into a conference room carrying a hammer. Very awkward. I started to hand it to the client.

"Oh, no," he said. He rolled back from the table and stuck his foot out. Did he mean for me to apply the hammer? Why, yes, he did.

The client sat in his chair with his foot out and held on to the edge of the table. I braced myself, bending my knees in my skirted blue suit, tilted the backside of the hammer around the offending nail and gave a yank.

"Oh, thank you so much."

"You're welcome, sir."

Upon Nick's return, I relayed the tale, complete with physical reenactment of the client rolling back from the table and sticking his foot out. We were hysterical. It was funny, but telling it revealed the true absurdity.

"You guys are fuckin' with me," Nick said, laughing. "No way."

"Way, baby." I handed him the nail. "Way."

Across the River

I dial our manufacturing plant in Secaucus for the thousandth time this week.

"This is Laura in New York. Is Joe Beronio around?"

"One minute."

He picks up.

"This is Joe… of the Jersey Beronios."

This place cracks me up.

Client From Another Time

8AM. The filing package was ready to go, I was just waiting for the attorney to come in and sign off. It was Amendment 1 for a small issuer, a tiny company really, the attorney was from a firm I'd never even heard of. The copies were all prepared, loose, the box to carry the package was in the room. The attorney was going to take a quick look to make sure everything was in order, sign off, and then we'd tape bind the books and fly the package man on board to DC. There was nothing unusual about this protocol. This job would be wrapped up by my ten o'clock smoke break. In and out.

When the attorney arrived I went to Room 6 to greet him and the first thing I noticed was the man didn't look like an attorney. Not a New York one, anyway. Well, not a New York one from this decade, I should clarify. He was wearing a thigh-length brown leather coat, the kind with wide lapels and a belt and big buttons, double-breasted—a coat I distinctly remember my father wearing when I was a child in the '70s. That, and he looked remarkably like Edward James Olmos, the actor who played the teacher in the '80s movie *Stand and Deliver*. He looked just like the character, down to the glasses and the uncomfortable comb-over. He was standing at the table by the filing package.

I gave him a quick rundown of the package: marked copies, clean copies, exhibits, the letter to the SEC.

"I'm sorry," he said. "I guess no one told you I need to blackline the document."

"It's blacklined, sir. You see here," I held up a marked copy with the obviously blacklined cover of Amendment 1 and flipped through it. "It's cumulatively blacklined from the original filing."

"No, I mean," he said, unbuttoning his anachronistic coat, "I like to blackline it myself."

Huh?

"I'm sorry?" I said.

"I need all the copies clean and I'll blackline them myself."

"By hand?" I said. "Are you sure, sir? That would take hours. You can trust our system, we have a process where we strip out all the marks after each filing and I can assure you this blackline's correct."

"I'm sure it is. I just like to do it." He took off his coat and hung it over the back of his chair. "And that's how I do it," he said, closing the topic.

He opened his weathered briefcase and pulled out a stack of original markup, presumably every change they had committed since the original filing; it looked like thirty or forty pages.

"It's okay," he said, "I can start with one of the clean ones."

Is he kidding?

He was not kidding. He settled in at the end of the table and pulled some supplies out of his case: a pen, a wooden ruler.

"Alright, sir, whatever you like."

"Thank you."

I went back to my desk shaking my head. I cut the work order to run more 8.5 x 11 clean and brought them to the room.

I was at my desk an hour or so later when my manager shouted over, "Melia, what's going on with your filing package? I've got Walter in DC, what time should he be meeting it?"

"It's gonna be a while," I called back.

I went to check on the client a few times; he never rang. I found him in the room, diligently working at the end of the table where I'd left him, his ruler on the page, referring to his original markup and then underlining the new sections of his document by hand, lifting the ruler away to mark tiny carets on the page with his black pen where things had been deleted. He asked me for a couple of new folios for ones he'd messed up.

Around lunchtime, I went in again (does he not realize we are trying to file this document TODAY?) but he seemed perfectly content, eating a sandwich, his chair turned toward the TV, watching the local news. Soon enough, the TV was off and he was back at work with his pen and ruler, me taping each book as he finished it, and then returning it to the room and putting it in the box, in what would come to be the slowest compilation of a filing package ever.

He finished his work, and when the box was all sealed up to go, I offered him a car.

"No, no, subway's fine," he said, waving me off. He put on his '70s trench coat, shook my hand, and thanked me. I watched him go down the hallway, his beaten old briefcase flopping beside him, this odd little client from another time. We flew the package to DC and filed it. It made the deadline, just six hours later than I'd predicted. I never saw the guy again... But I never forgot him either.

Soaked

A light rain turned into a torrential downpour this morning.

Making my way from the apartment of last night's hook up, the subway flooded and I had to get off at Canal Street. Trudging north with a useless umbrella I tuck into a doorway for some relief. Three other people are already in it. We wait five minutes, squashed together in city-solidarity, a wall of water bouncing off the sidewalk into our ledge. The rain's not letting up at all. I check my watch and make a run for it.

I arrive at work fully drenched. Every dayside rep is soaked to the skin. Soggy pants and blazers, shoes ruined. It's spring, most of us didn't even have jackets. We're fifteen wet dogs.

The manager brings two boxes from Sales and we work all morning in bare feet and sales promo attire—golf shirts and button-downs sporting our company logo.

It felt like camp.

Asia, Alaska

"So, you know how Cover 2's supposed to be a map of Asia?"

"Yeah," the guy from Manufacturing says into the phone.

"Well, we're lookin' at the printed sample and, uh… it's not a map of Asia."

"Okay," he says slowly.

"It's a map of… ALASKA."

"What?!"

"They both do start with the letter A, so there's that."

"Holy shit, you're right. FUCK!"

"Did you already ship?"

"Lemme check, I'll call you back."

"I'm sure this'll be funny a few years from now."

"Shit. You gonna wanna reprint?"

"Um, yeah."

London

Oh my god, is that my alarm? I peek out from my covers to the clock that sits on the wicker hamper that serves as my night table. 10AM. Oh no, it's too early. I work nights, barely been asleep six hours.

Wait, it's not the alarm, it's the phone. The phone is ringing. God, who is calling this early? It can only be work.

I flip my arm out from under my non-duveted down comforter, slap around for the receiver and pull it back into bed with me.

"Hello?" I mumble.

"Laura? It's Chris." One of the managers. I hear phones ringing and the noises of the Customer Service Department behind him. Voices in the distance.

"Hey."

"Good morning, sunshine!" he says.

"Good morning," I say. I hope I didn't fuck something up last night.

"So listen, you have a passport, right?"

"Yeah."

"What are you doing this weekend?"

Ugh. Loaded question.

"Uhh…"

"We have a Rick Russell job that wants to come in house in London, can you work it?" Rick Russell's a salesman.

"I guess so, what job is it?"

"I don't have all the information yet. He wants a New York rep there. So, you can go?"

"Yeah."

"Okay, I'll call you back with more info."

"Alright."

"Talk to you later," he says.

"Bye." I push the phone out and rock it back into its cradle. Roll over and go back to sleep.

RING.

"Hello?"

I'm still in bed. I eye the clock. 11:15.

"Hey, it's Chris."

"Hey."

"So here's the deal with that job," he says. Jesus, can't this wait till I come in this afternoon?

"Mm-hm," I mumble.

"A car is going to pick you up at one o'clock."

I'm suddenly awake.

"What??"

"I said: a car is going to pick you up at one o'clock."

"I thought this job was for the weekend! One o'clock? That's like," I look at the clock again, "not even two hours from now."

"Is that a problem?"

I close my eyes. Pause.

"Okay. One o'clock." I say. "How many days should I pack for?"

"It could be three days, maybe three weeks, I don't know."

"How am I supposed to pack for that??"

"Just bring three days and if it's longer you get it dry cleaned."

"Oh my god," I say, sitting up in bed. "Alright. What job is it? How do I get my tickets?"

"We're still putting the info together. The driver will have a package for you."

I call my mom, pack a bag. At 1PM sharp I look out my window and a town car is parked by my curb.

The driver did indeed have a package for me. A large white envelope with our company name stamped on it. As we roll down the block away from my apartment I open it.

Inside the package is a copy of the document, the working group list, a one-way ticket to London, a few post-its with the name of a hotel and the address of our London office, and an envelope with $1000 cash. I felt like I was on *Mission Impossible*.

I take a closer look at the working group list.

"Can I use your phone?" I ask the driver as we get on the highway.

I dial the New York Managers' desk.

"Hey, it's Laura," I say when he picks up.

"What happened, isn't he there yet?"

"Yeah, that's fine, I'm in the car already," I say. "But this working group list—are you fuckin' with me?"

"Whaddaya talkin' about?"

"The main attorney is Oliver W. Holmes? The colorwork contact is Armand Assante?"

He laughs. "Really?" he says, "I don't know, I got the list from the team. You want me to check?"

I flip through the list for the bankers. Tom Jones heads the page. Gimme a break.

"No, it's fine, whatever," I say. Oliver Wendell fucking Holmes. These fucking guys.

"Call in when you get to the office and see what's what."

"Alright."

"Have a good trip," he says.

"Thanks."

Around midnight London time, I check into the hotel. Compared to an American hotel, the place practically looks like it's closed. Lobby lights all dimmed; London was already using energy conservation measures unheard of in the States. I step off the elevator into a dark hallway toward my room and motion sensors activate the lights ahead of me as I walk.

I get a poor night's sleep and take a subpar shower in the morning, the water pressure the equivalent of standing in the rain. A breakfast entailing a sparse selection of breads and potato. Fruit? Egg? Coffee? Meats? No, sorry, you entitled American. Welcome to Europe.

This was my first time overseas and I had no sense of the city layout at all. I was convinced the cab was taking advantage of my lack of knowledge, seemingly driving around in circles, roundabout after roundabout, before pulling up to our office.

From the street, our London office looked like a brownstone. Lovely, really. Inside I went through the customary meet and greet, putting faces to all the operations folks I knew by name or voice. They had a fridge with free snacks and mini-meals, an extensive tea set-up, a multi-floor layout with a number of conference rooms, windows in Customer Service! It was all very civilized, no one was yelling or running. Still no coffee however, which was a grave disappointment.

I set up the job, prepared for the in-house. About 10AM the first client arrived.

I went to the conference room to introduce myself. I guessed I was on my own with this jerked up working group list.

"Good morning," I said, coming around the table. I put my business card on the table as the client fiddled his own card out of his wallet.

"I'm Laura Melia, from Bowne of New York," I said, holding my hand out for a shake.

"Nice to meet you, Laura," he said, shaking my hand. "Ollie Holmes."

I looked down at his card on the table.

Oliver W. Holmes, it stated, in Garamond font.

And then Ollie Holmes and I worked that deal straight through. Forty-one consecutive hours in the office; the longest straight shift I ever worked. Thank god for the mini-meals. Really coulda used the coffee.

Teamwork

"We just got another," Joe says, hanging up the phone. "This night is crazy."

Half the floor is being renovated so our team is squashed in a back room separated from the rest of Customer Service.

"You guys look a little cramped in here," a maintenance guy says happening by our open doorway.

"Ya think?" a colleague says. Active jobs are stacked on top of each other, we'd completely run out of space.

Joe's already on the phone to alert the kitchen of the additional in-house. "Yeah, we got another group coming in, Banco Popular, 3 people, 8PM." He pauses. "I know! But they're coming."

"I got a guy looking at a bookproof in 15, he should be outta here by eight," I say.

The maintenance guy looked around the room: two makeshift counters already covered with in-house deals, fax games ganged up in overlapping piles along the edge of the room. I'm bumping up a job on top of another job on my desk.

"Where you gonna set up another in-house?" he said, stating the obvious. When a group comes in-house, you need some counter space to set up: the master, a Bates stamper, the log sheet for pages, pre-run copies of fax cover sheets, a hit sheet for recording faxes and photocopies, and other paperwork for the deal. The set up is typically four to six piles.

"Yeah, no shit," a rep said, bustling out of the room past him, hands full of pages.

The maintenance guy stepped further into the room. Eyed our doorway. Put his hands on his hips. More pages are coming out of the printer, I go over to see which job it is.

"Laur, you got Sharon in Phoenix on 8-2."

"I've got an idea," Maintenance says, to no one in particular.

"Hey, Shar, what's up?" I say, picking up my call.

The phone is ringing again. "New York Customer Service," another colleague answers as the maintenance guy wanders out.

BzzzBING! We all look at the board. 19.

I cut a work order for Xerox and bring a proof back there for them to run for the FedEx deadline. I rush back to my desk.

"Laur, Jim Sherry holding on 8-0."

"Thanks," I say.

The maintenance guy appears again, crouching on the floor in the doorway. Whatever, we can't stop to see what every fucking person is doing.

"Laura Melia," I say, picking up my client.

Soon more pages are coming out of the printer. I hang up with my client and pull my changed pages out from the pile and log them back to my master.

BzzzBING! 21. That's me. Out the door to bring CPOs to the conference room, making a copy of the fresh pages on my way. Hurry back again.

The maintenance guy is fiddling with the top of the door now, what's he got, a screwdriver?

I peel a post-it off my computer.

"Laur, John Pinto from Lehman on 8-1, and you need to call back Hal in DC."

"Okay," I say.

The maintenance guy now had his arms spread across our door, it's detached and he's moving it, side stepping it into our room.

"Gimme a hand," he calls out.

"Laura Melia," I say, picking up the Lehman call on 8-1.

With the help of another guy, he lays the door across two filing cabinets at the side of the room, instantly forming another countertop for us.

"Yes, John, what can I do for you?"

"Oh my god, this is amazing," someone says.

"Thank you so much," says another. Jobs and papers fill the new counter like algae spreading in fast forward.

BzzzBING! 13.

Ring, ring. "New York Customer Service."

"No problem, guys." The maintenance guy brushes off his hands and smiles at us. "Teamwork."

We're back in business without a beat.

On In-Houses

Client at the counter on Day 4 of an in-house.

Client: "If you see me here tomorrow, kill me."

Rep: "Okay... but we're gonna have to charge you for that."

Intercom

Anyone can page anyone, that's how our system's set up. Punch a few numbers on your phone and—BAM—you're connected into the overhead intercom speaker that broadcasts across our floors.

It's necessary, and typically not abused, but in the evenings the protocol sometimes gets a little… lax.

"Ted Bernadelli to Team A, Ted Bernadelli to Team A," someone announces a few minutes before midnight. Ted comes into view, waddling through the hallway that separates the two sides of the department. He's about 25 feet from his destination (Team A) when someone else clicks into the announcement system.

"Ted Bernadelli to Team B, Ted Bernadelli to Team B." Ted stops in his tracks.

"C'mon," he says. Team B is on the other side of the department and I see him debating whether to continue to his original destination or backtrack to his new one.

A beep comes over the speaker, someone else is calling in testing the intercom by pressing a number.

"Ted Bernadelli to the 9th Floor vending machine, Ted Bernadelli—9th Floor vending." A round of chuckles as Ted aborts his mission and returns to his home team.

My Feet Are Bleeding

The in-houses had us running. Forth, with pages: carpet, rubber, tile, carpet. Back, with markup: carpet, tile, rubber, carpet. To the counter, to the Xerox machine, to the fax, to the printer. Back to the Xerox, and again, to the conference room.

A rep from Cleveland was in town.

"Is it like this EVERY DAY?" he said when we met at the Xerox machine.

"Pretty much," I said, putting my pages into the bin.

"This in-house is killing me, they're ringing like every ten minutes. The clients in Cleveland are much more relaxed."

"Ha! I bet they are," I said. I tapped a few buttons on the screen to get my copies going. "How many conference rooms you have in Cleveland?"

"Three."

"Come on, dude. I'm workin' three just by myself," I ribbed over the noise.

"It's the walking, the amount of walking you guys do here is nuts."

"You get used to it," I said.

"Laura, you don't understand," he said as my copies stopped. "My feet... are BLEEDING."

I smiled. He was a nice guy, round and jovial, a potential poster boy for Cleveland—to me, anyway, since he was the only person I'd ever met from Cleveland.

"Yeah," I said, pulling my copies and originals off the machine. This is New York, man, do you think bleeding feet impress us?

"BLEEDING, Laura, I'm not kidding!"

I stepped around him. We do not react to mere bleeding feet.

"My feet are literally bleeding from this in-house," he said to the display screen as he put his pages in.

"Try doin' it in heels, tough guy," I said, walking away.

His laugh followed me.

"You guys are all fucking crazy!" he called after me.

I spun and walked backwards for a few steps, my arms outstretched with pages, and gave him a wide smile.

"Welcome to New York!"

And You Call Everyone

Oh, the calls.

You field calls from typesetting sites all night long. Every few minutes Composition is calling for someone on the team. They're waiting for your job, do you have an ETA? They got the job but they're missing a page. They got the page but it's cut off. The page is clear but they can't read the client's handwriting. They can read the client's handwriting but they don't understand what the client is trying to indicate. They know what the markup is indicating but it's referencing something they're missing. They completely understand the client's markup but they have a question about an inconsistency the markup is intending to implement. They're working on the client's markup but it's running late. They've successfully worked the markup and they're sending it back to you, they need a device to output to. They want to know if they can close the job out yet.

You field calls from manufacturing sites all night long. They know your job's coming, can you confirm the specs? The job you have that's printing next week, what will the paper stock be?

When do the clients want books? Do you have the quantity? Is that job a separate cover or self? What color is the logo? They have the timing for your job. They're waiting for your job, do you have an ETA? The job's on bookproof, do you know when it's going to clear? They heard the job cleared, are you sending the work order? They got the work order but they're missing the file. They got the file but they're missing the work order. They opened the file and it's got problems. They got the work order and the files, but are missing the distro. The job's off press, they're sending samples. They have your POD.

You field calls from clients all night long. They're sending pages. They're looking for pages. They're looking for a copy of the filing from August 28th. They have distribution instructions. They're sending more pages. Where are their pages? They're getting ready to file and need the submission. They're sending you a letter for the SEC. They're OK to File. Did the filing get accepted? Did the as-filed distribution go out? They're sending more pages. Can they get a blackline from how the document looked three weeks ago at 10PM? Where are their pages? Did you get their fax? Their package? Can you send a proof to Chicago? To San Fransisco? To a vacation home in Boca Raton? To Frankfurt and Hong Kong? Can they all get there by 9AM local times? They're going to try to print on Wednesday. They're planning to come in-house on Monday. They're sending a few more pages. Can they get a copy of the distribution from the prelim? Where are their fucking pages?! Did the bankers send you all the distro yet? Did the attorneys stop submitting changes yet? They're ready to bookproof. They need to bust a page on the bookproof. They're OK to Print. Where are their books? Can they get a few more books? How about a POD?

You get calls from salespeople, calls from the kitchen, calls from other reps, other sites and departments.

And you call everyone. Can you take my pages? I'm sending you pages. Where are my pages? How fast can you get it to me? I just spoke to him. As soon as possible. Did you get what I sent you? They'll be here at eight. Where are my pages? Rider 6B's not in the file? Forty thousand for locals Thursday. I'm sending it right now. You still got room on the overnight for 6AM? I'm returning your call. How fast can you turn it? When do you think you'll send it? It's mostly text, I swear. Five people, ten o'clock. I'm sending more pages. I'm sorry, sir. Yes. Absolutely. Hold on, lemme check. Typesetting, please. I told them twelve hours but it's really eight to ten. Can you take my pages? It should be there shortly. No, it's for a filing. They busted a page. It's for the morning. It's for noon tomorrow. It's a rush. Which job are we talking about? Blue 286. I need a POD. I need an affidavit. I need a car, body uptown. Hey, yeah, I really need that timing now. I'll try to buy you an hour, but I definitely need it by five. It's cleared. It's coming. It's OK to File. It's OK to Print. Are the locals out? Thank you. You're welcome. Who told you that? And where are my fucking pages?

Have a Cookie

"Jesus Christ, will this night ever stop?" I say as my phone rings again.

"Laura Melia," I answer.

"LM." The girl from the kitchen has developed a habit of calling me by my initials, the way I'm identified on the team note beside the jobs I'm assigned to. It's endearing actually, a small badge of honor in this crazy place. "One of your clients in 13 asked for a breakout. I put him in 2."

"Okay, thanks," I say.

BzzzBING! I look to the board as I hang up. 2.

I'm buried. Two in-houses, three fax games, at least a dozen other active deals on the go, I try to predict what my client in Room 2 wants, no idea, I don't even know who it is. In a futile effort to stay one step ahead of the never-ending wave of work, I grab a set of pages going back to my other conference room.

"Laur, you got Toronto on 8-3," a colleague says.

"Tell 'em I'll call 'em back," I say, pushing back from my desk. I head to the hallway, hustling. I drop my pages at my other conference room and continue down the hallway to Room 2.

I swing open the door to Room 2 and see my main attorney sitting at the boardroom table. He's my favorite on this deal. A pudgy Spanish gentleman in his 30s. Strange he'd take a break-out though, the main attorney normally sticks with the group.

"Laura," he says in his Spanish accent.

"Can I help you?" I switch off the buzzer.

"Busy night tonight," he says. Yeah, it's busy alright. His group's over twenty people, they've been here a few days already, working toward filing and printing. Not to mention all the other deals I've got working. We're slammed.

"Yes, very busy," I say.

"It was time to step away from the chaos for a moment, maybe you would like to join me," he says.

"I'm sorry?" I say. What's going on here?

"Have a cookie," he says. It is then I notice the platter of chocolate chip cookies on the conference room table. The signature ones we get from our local vendor, baked in the Village with big chunky chips. He's got an entire platter of them on the table. How'd he get a whole platter of cookies in here so fast?

"Oh, thanks," I say, still holding the door about to exit. "But I've really got to get back. Is there anything I can help you with?" I do love those cookies, but I can practically hear the pile of work accruing on my desk every second that ticks by. Eating a cookie? Not a priority right now.

"Sit," he says. "One cookie."

It's hard to say no to a client.

"Okay," I say.

I sit across from him, the tray of cookies between us.

He takes a cookie. I take one. The room is silent.

I bite into my cookie and start chewing. He's chewing too. It's completely uncomfortable. I'm wondering if my other conference rooms are ringing. Are their numbers up on the board right now, buzzing unanswered? What did the rep in Toronto want?

"We have to take a moment every now and then," the attorney says. I take another bite.

"Mm," I say, mouth full of cookie, wholly distracted. Am I supposed to be having a conversation with him? I stare at the plate of 10-12 cookies and feel his dark eyes watching me. This is totally weird. Is he planning to eat all these cookies? They are very filling. You can only eat a couple, even if you're really hungry. Is this harassment? Room 2 is right near the receptionist, it's okay, I decide.

"Slow down," he says. Slowing down is impossible right now, something akin to hopping on the track at the Daytona 500 with a stop sign. I wonder if the pages for my fax games are laying on the printer, being shuffled over by other reps, maybe getting lost. I'm chewing for what seems like an eternity, imagining post-its piling up on my computer as one phone call after another goes un-fielded. I take a final bite.

"Sometimes you just need to eat a cookie," he says. I give him a smile that I hope doesn't look as fake as it feels. This is the worst cookie I've ever eaten. And these are normally very good cookies. I have to get out of here.

"Thanks so much, Francisco," I say, getting up from the table. "This was very kind of you."

"Time," he says. "We can never get it back." He takes another cookie from the tray.

"You're right," I say, pulling the door closed behind me. "Lemme know if you need anything."

I hurry back toward my team, arms swinging. I didn't hear anything he said.

Cornermark 274

It was a long day. The latest of many long days in a series of many long weeks. We were busy, so busy. At 1AM I found my dinner (the bottom half of a tin of spaghetti) smashed between two proofs and a job bag as I was turning over to Tino.

"What the——?" he said, throwing the proofs in the trash.

I shrugged.

"I guess I forgot about it," I said.

We worked so many pages, faxing out, faxing back, re-faxing. The re-faxing was the worst; no one likes having to go backwards to go forwards.

A half hour later I was in my car heading down to Walker's for a drink. Stopped at a light on Varick, numb in the silent daze of my car, there was honking. At first I ignored it, but when the honking continued I finally looked around. Another rep was in the car next to me. Waving his cigarette in the dark, he signaled for me to roll down my window. I obliged; we were heading to the same place.

"Hey!" he yelled, "Sharon wants you to re-fax cornermark

274!!" He burst into laughter in the glow of the red light. I cracked up.

The light changed and he sped ahead of me.

Hale-Bopp

It's busy season 1997 and we're just getting killed, night after night.

Everyone's running. We do not pee, we do not eat, we do not get a drink of water. All we do is the next thing. As fast as fucking possible, with zero error allowance. The next thing. The next thing. The next thing.

We're stressed. And, sure, we're angry. But we don't have time for evolved emotion. Instead we fume while we do the next thing. We compensate with random cursing and not-so-random outbursts. We slam our phone receivers down or dump a stack of proofs into our tall garbage can with a force that leaves the can wobbling in our wake. We yell at the manager and then stomp off to do the next thing.

The Hale-Bopp suicides are in the news and someone's blown up the cover of the *NY Post* and hung it on a pillar in Customer Service.

"THEY DIED IN SHIFTS," it reads, across a pair of Nike sneakers.

Car 109

"Sir, no, he should be there already. It's Car 109," I say into the phone. "You don't see him? Look for a town car, his number'll be in the window. Car 109... Okay, hold on a second." I put the client on hold.

"Remind me to thank dayside for setting up this asinine fucking pickup," I say to my colleague across the desk as I dial the Traffic Department. Who tells the client to meet the driver with a package instead of having the driver go up?

"Kenny, it's Laura. Can you get me Intaboro 109 on the phone?" I put Traffic on hold. Pick up the client line.

"Sir, yes, please bear with me, I'm getting the driver on the other line." I put the client back on hold.

"You got him yet, Kenny? I got the client holding."

"I hate this fuckin' shit," I say to my colleague. He gives me a look of sympathy and hands me a post-it across the counter between us. It reads, "Tell Dayside THEY SUCK!!!" I laugh under my breath.

"You're a true friend, you know that?" I say as I stick it to my computer. He winks.

"Kenny? Okay, thanks." He connects me.

"Hello? Yes, are you Intaboro 109? Are you at 85 Broad yet?... Are you inside or outside?... What part of the street? My guy is looking for you and can't find you... No, it's for a package, not a body... Is your number in the window?... Okay, hold on a second."

"Sir, he's there. One-oh-nine, yes. He's on the west side of the street closer to Stone. Look for 109 in the window... It's okay, I'll hold, sir."

I cover the mouthpiece and say to my colleague, "This is SO not okay. This is what I'm doing with my $80,000 education, dude."

"Yes, okay, sir, hold on a second."

"Driver, can you see my guy? He's looking for you, can you get out of your car?... Sorry, what?... What does he LOOK like?"

I roll my eyes at my colleague.

"Oh, I don't know, white guy, six feet tall, wearing a suit, wandering around in front of 85 Broad with a package like he's looking for a driver??" I press the receiver to my blazer.

"I've just described 90% of the people in the financial district," I say to my colleague. He open-mouth laughs.

"109, I have no idea what he looks like. Hold on a sec, okay?"

My colleague lifts his chin at me.

"Laur," he says in a serious tone, "I hate to tell you this but he's never gonna find him… there's something you don't know about Car 109."

I stare at him, my hand over the receiver with my two calls on hold.

"What?" I say.

"Car 109…," he says.

69

I wait.

"The driver…," he says.

"Yeah, WHAT??"

He leans in toward the counter with a deadpan face.

"Car 109's the Invisible Man."

We laugh until we cry.

Jose Blanco

Meeting Joe was like the best of college. Like college was when you found your people—those friends who think in all the same fucked up ways that you do.

We're in midtown at a comped company event, leaning against a huge pillar in the reception area having a cocktail.

It seems like years since I started, but it's probably only two years.

Years since I arrived on his team and he said, "Thank god you're here! I was starting to get a complex about my ass," spinning his skinny frame and nodding to the two Dominican members of the team who were gratuitously blessed in the rear.

Maybe longer since I asked, "Can I use this phone to call my boyfriend?" and he said over his shoulder, "We call Caracas at the drop of a hat, yeah, I think you can call New Jersey."

He taught me how to be a rep. How to write a work order.

"Okay, now, in the Comments: spell it all out for them again. This is typesetting. Spell it out for them like they're five."

Ages since the floor was under construction, and we'd head to an alcove, behind a half-finished wall of drywall in the future client lounge, smoking and putting our butts into the empty soda can left by smokers who came before us.

Years since he said nonchalantly between smokes, "You know I'm gay, right?"

"Yeah," I said, even though I didn't.

At least a year after the company gave us tickets to *Rent*, and when the final curtain called, I said, "I don't know whether I wanna elope or kill myself."

He laughed and said, "I fucking love you."

In a few years, he'd leave to work at a start-up and I'd be the nightside Production Manager. But tonight we're reps. Fast friends, and Customer Service Reps.

It's still years before he'd break me out of Saint Vincent's Hospital, after I collapsed from heartbreak in a bar on Seventh Avenue.

A lifetime since I took a shower in his Hell's Kitchen apartment, which sported a free-standing bathtub in the middle of its kitchen. Pulling the black curtain around, I said, "It's like the Batcave in here!"

Maybe just before the time we got stoned in my apartment and he asked, "If you had to choose between a great relationship and a great job, which would you pick?"

"A relationship, of course!"

"Really?" he said, "I'd never have guessed that."

It was around the time his car was stolen in The Village. Or actually, not stolen, just taken for a joyride and returned to the same parking spot it had been in—except facing the other direction.

"Hey, at least they brought it back," he said.

There's a million stories in the naked city, and Joe White had

999,999 of them.

I don't remember what the event was or why we were there.

It's just a day since the last time he said, "Melia!" with the phone in his ear to the diner downstairs, "Fries?"

Months after we were driving somewhere and turning onto the highway entrance ramp I said, "Do you ever think you're like that because you feel guilty about your mom?"

Slapping my dashboard, he exclaimed, "Oh my god! That's totally it! See! You don't need a shrink if you have a friend!"

Weeks since I had an affair with a guy from the train.

"What do you think I should do?" I'd asked when it became a possibility.

"Go for it," he said, "Worse comes to worst, it'll make a good story."

He was right. It did, and still does.

It's maybe four years before the afternoon, in the bar PJs across the street, after I'd grumbled for ten minutes about my inability to find a serious relationship, he said, "You know what your problem is? You've got too many loose ends. You're still sleeping with guys you dated years ago." He took a drag of his smoke.

"I like to have options," I said.

"You've got too many options. Ex-boyfriends, ex-lovers, random hookups, all these guys you already know are going nowhere. Start tying up these loose ends and then you'll be open to actually meeting someone real." He took a sip of his drink while I considered.

"Yeah, but then…," I said, "who would I sleep with?"

He slapped his hand down on the bar.

"Damn it, girl!" And then punctuating each word with another slap, "TIE! 'EM! UP!"

It took me almost a year to tie up all those loose ends. Three months after I did I met my husband.

But tonight we're here. Hundreds of beers into our relationship, so many nights at The North River, The Ear, The Emerald, a million laughs, uncountable cigarettes, thousands of turnovers behind us and thousands more to come, we're dolled up for tonight's event. I lean against the pillar and give him a stare as I take a sip of my drink.

"That look though…," he says as I peek up from behind the mascara I never wear to work. "You almost turned ME on."

Good Morning, Gentlemen

"They been here all night," the third shift rep turned his in-house to me in his Bronx accent. "Main group's in 11, usin' 10 as a breakout. I woke 'em up at 6:30 for showers an' breakfast. A few went home overnight an' are due back by 9. Job's been C2'd an' you got a fresh work order open in Phoenix, but—in case any questions from last night—I didn't put the pricing copy through yet." He patted the stack of pages containing the photocopy of every change the clients had submitted in the last 24 hours, all bound up with our required paperwork, a copy of yesterday's work order, and the telltale pink sheets for the counts of how many photocopies and faxes had been done on behalf of the in-house. Just like attorneys, we bill for everything.

"Thanks," I said.

"You got 20 proofs runnin' in the back for 8AM," he continued. We both instinctively looked up at the wall clock labeled New York, sitting cozily between London and Chicago. 07:50, it read. "Should be done any minute."

"Tryin' to file and print today?"

Tino nodded. "Yep." He placed his hand on the SEC submission set up with the in-house. "Sub headers been updated." He riffled a pile of memos and greensheets and slid it from his side of the counter to mine. "Print distro done for what we have so far. You're still waitin' for Lehman and the working group. Run is 20,000 with a 16-hour turn."

He'd handwritten "Missing Lehman + Wkg Grp" on the first page of the distribution, with a big circle around it so there was no confusion. Tino and I turned like butter, but you never know who's gonna pick up your job. In Customer Service 16 hours of your day are controlled by other people; you learn to cover your ass.

"You're a rockstar. Anything else?"

"That's it." He turned his big belly away from the counter and back toward the desk we shared. Loosened his tie. "Oh, and tell nightside we're done bein' their bitch for breakin' down labels. My guys musta broke 30,000 labels last night."

"Ahh, the third shift lament."

"Yeah, look, you know we'll do it, but we don't like doin' it if they just leave it for us 'cause…," he waved his hand ambiguously, "…they don't feel like it."

"Got it."

He picked up his keys.

"See ya tomorrow."

"Later, T," I said.

I moved all my job bags to my desk and checked the clock. 07:55, time to see how the proofs for my in-house were doing. I walked to Shipping and found them on the proofs counter, ready to go. I slid them off the edge of the counter, leaning the stack against my body, curling my fingers around the far edge of the bottom proofs to get some leverage. One thing about this job, you build up some arm muscles.

I headed out of Shipping and made a direct line for my conference room, taking the ramp behind the managers' desks. I needed two hands to carry a proof stack that large, so when I got to the hallway door, I backed into it, pushing the handle down with my elbow. Down the hallway, I reached the closed door of Conference Room 11. Same procedure: my hands full, I depressed the handle with my elbow and backed into the room.

Turning around, I saw the clients. A dozen men in various stages of undress, getting ready for the day. A couple of the guys were in undershirts, putting their dress shirts on. One tying his necktie. One still in boxer shorts, stepping into a pair of pants, one in his unbuckled suit bottom pulling a white t-shirt over his hairy chest.

"Good morning, gentlemen!" I said, at a comedic shout. A few nervous laughs and smiles. One guy was on the couch tying his shoe. He looked down the edge of the room as I placed the proofs on the corner of the table.

"This is quite scandalous. See what happens when you're five minutes early?" he said, shirt unbuttoned and tie hanging loose around his neck.

I took my master off the top of the proof stack and reached behind me to pull the door closed as I stepped out the way I came. Legs in the hallway, I bent my head in through the door opening.

"No offense, but as far as scandals go," I swept the room with my eyes, "you guys gotta step up your game."

I closed the door on them laughing and click-clacked my way back to Customer Service. The day was off to a good start.

J. Cameron Keane

J. Cameron Keane was A Professional Corporation.

At least that's what it said in our Rolodex, where he was listed under his own name as the company, with himself as his only employee, and his address as the Soho Grand Hotel in downtown Manhattan.

J. Cameron Keane was actually from San Fransisco. Whether he found our California offices too slow, too sunny, or whether he simply preferred a New York adventure when he worked his document, I can't say, but he always came alone and unannounced. Easy-going, he'd arrive empty-handed, save a number of a San Fran job, and he'd leave empty-handed, keeping not a trace of evidence that he had been in-house at all.

J. Cameron Keane was slim and tan, dressed casually in his west coast suit, maybe mid-50s, with gold hair brushed straight back from his forehead, and he liked the color green. Would only mark up his documents with green pen. Had all his books taped in green. He worked on documents for companies you've never heard of, and he loved to drink. J. Cameron Keane would drink vodka all day if you let him. And, of course, we let him.

"Cam Keane's here. He's in 18," the dayside rep turned to me. "Don't light a match in the conference room."

J. Cameron Keane was a pleasant drunk, courteous and kind, totally functional, and always wrapped it up by 7PM when he would order a car and disappear to an actual drinking establishment. He had a photographic memory, calling in without fail later the same evening, the sounds of a noisy bar behind him.

"I've been thinking about page 48 of the document. The third paragraph, second sentence is it?" He'd say the sentence as I flipped madly to the page in the proof. "Change the word to 'intended,' would you? Thanks, love."

J. Cameron Keane was a mystery. One time the car service said they drove him all around the city, waiting for him outside various addresses, uptown, downtown, until finally depositing him at the airport where he boarded a flight to Ireland and asked the car to wait 24 hours for his return. He did return. And he went right back to the Soho Grand.

On Turnover

"Petrosemex."

"I'll be honest with ya," the dayside rep smiled sideways as he shuffled the job bag up for turnover. "I haven't looked at this bag since 8AM."

We both laugh. His hair was a mess, I could tell it must have been a rough day.

"Okay," I said, taking the bag. "How 'bout Daimler?"

Prelims and Finals

"So, we'll be in Wednesday to work toward clearing the final," the attorney says.

"Okay. About how many people will you be?" I say into the phone.

"Eight."

"And around what time?"

"Around six."

"Alright." I check my notes. "Are you still looking at a run of 18,000?"

"That sounds right," he says.

"Okay. We've received distribution instructions from Salomon but no one else."

"I'll follow up with the underwriters," he says.

"Great, thanks," I say.

"Oh, and one other thing," the attorney says.

I wait.

"It'd be good if for the final you could print the logo right side up."

WHAT?

"Sorry?" I say, scrambling in the job bag for a sample of the prelim. I pull it out, it's a doughnut-shaped logo.

"Yeah, it printed upside-down on the preliminary," he says.

I flip the book around, flip it back the other way. Shit, it does look different. Just slightly, barely noticeable, but different. Fuck.

"Absolutely. We'll fix that right away," I say. "Definitely right side up for the final."

Nice Tie

"Nice tie," I say to Dean as we pass each other in the hallway.

"You're like the third person to compliment me on this tie today," he says, slowing down.

"Oh yeah?"

"Yeah, a girl bought it for me and whenever I wear it I always get compliments. People are like, 'Hey, Dean, nice tie. Hey Dean, love your tie.'"

"She has good taste," I say.

"And then when I wear a tie I bought myself people are like, 'Yep, there's Dean.'"

I laugh and we go on our ways.

Call My Wife

The client had been awake for days—three full days and after midnight of his third night in house—when his legs gave out as he was standing at the Customer Service counter. He collapsed, dropping onto the ceramic floor of the hallway and cracking his head open during the nightside shift turnover.

There was blood.

"Call the kitchen!" someone yelled, which in financial print is who you call for pretty much any issue that can't be solved by Customer Service. The kitchen staff came running from the opposite side of the building; Sean Carter zipped by with handfuls of white towels. Someone phoned an ambulance.

A small crowd gathered on the floor around the guy, and his CS rep leaned over him.

"Sir?"

"Call my wife," he told her.

His colleagues were directly across the hall in Conference Room 7. The client at the end of the table leaned back, looked out, closed the door to their conference room Godfather-style, and then rang the bell to ask where their pages were while this other guy was lying in the hallway.

The client had surgery and slowly recovered. Months later he returned to work.

"He's back," his rep told me, when we caught up on the news during turnover. "But I don't know…"

She absentmindedly straightened some papers around the job we were turning.

"What?" I said. She shook her head.

"He's not the same."

Thank You, Sir

Everyone has that client. That first regular client who makes you feel like you're doing something here, something important—who's big enough, high-profile enough the salesperson wants *you*, it's important it's *you* working their deal. That client that comes back again and again, over the course of years, so much so that you become a true extension of the working group.

You see the attorneys from their law firm mature and advance, the new associates taken off-guard by your intimate knowledge of the account.

"Saturday delivery? No problem. Should we send it to the Manhattan apartment or to his house in New Canaan?"

You know how the clients like to work, you can predict their distribution instructions, prompting a forgotten name. You recite job details from memory, dial the phone numbers of key players by heart. You don't need to ask the client for specs. You know their paper stock, the color of their logo, you look at a list of names and know who's on the Board of Directors, who's the partner from the law firm.

In reality it's just your ego. You are only a tiny cog, oblivious to the larger picture of their business activities or motives, your salary and status dwarfed by the moguls of the working group. In reality, you are merely a peripheral character in the drama of their deal, a walk-on role not even mentioned in the final credits.

But, damn, it feels good when the big man from the company stands up at the head of the conference room table and shouts to his group: "Settle down, everybody, and listen up! Laura's going to tell us how we'll get it done."

He sits back in his chair and the room quiets. You lay out the plan for how they'll get books around the world in the next 48 hours.

"You heard her, that's our timeline," he says to his group. "Now, let's get it done."

He gives you a nod and you take your leave, softly closing the door behind you. You clack down the dimmed hallway and you feel part of something, something important.

Just a tiny part… but that's something.

Tech Support

I call IT in a frenzy: "We got problems on BNY_PS3, it's makin' all kinds of crazy noises, get over here!"

He comes over and after briefly inspecting the renegade printer, he says in his halting English, "Laura. You hear these noises. This printer is saying to you: I am old."

I stare at him.

"Power off, power on," he says, pressing the button before scurrying back to his cube.

Urban Legends

Every industry has its urban legends, and financial print is no different.

The clients were in-house for weeks and one of the law firms brought a proofreader with them. The working group was so mean to this guy, treated him like shit for the weeks they were in house. Finally, when they were getting ready to file, they left the proofreader reading pages until all hours of the night. The guy was so pissed, he'd finally had it. When the group arrived in the morning to file the job, they found a set of clean proofs in the conference room, and a note that read: "I inserted seven curse words into your document. Good luck finding them."

The attorneys read the document for hours and found six. They could never find the seventh. Was it there or not?

This client gave the rep hell all year long. Not even regular stuff, this client was evil, a true sadist. Eventually the rep had enough and sent a box of dog shit to the client's house.

Need to passive aggressively respond to a client who's driving you crazy? Slide a piece of black paper around the roll of a fax machine and tape it to its own end in a loop. Dial the client's number. The client will get a perpetual stream of black coming out on their side, effectively using up all their toner.

A client came in one night, completely bombed, insisting on working the document. The guy was so trashed, the rep called the partner and delicately explained he didn't think it was a good idea for the guy to be marking up the proof in that condition. A deal was struck: the document was cloned into another file and the guy worked on the "document" all night, including giving an OK to File which the team mocked up an SEC acceptance for just to get the guy to finally leave.

A female rep went into a conference room to find the entire (male) working group watching a porn movie.

Come to think of it, all of these things might have happened. Or not. It's hard to say with urban legends.

Mexico City

I was on my first trip to Mexico City. Our office there was like a garden oasis; just two stories, with an open-air courtyard separating the conference rooms from the Customer Service room and the rest of the workspaces—so different than New York. I sat in on a client meeting with the General Manager. Afterwards he took me aside.

"Laura," he said in his Spanish accent, which had a lovely way of highlighting the u in my name. "There's something you need to know about doing business in Mexico." We stood near the door of the courtyard, flowers blooming. His black hair was waxed into a neat coif, comb lines visible.

"Okay," I said.

"How do I say this…? Think of the meeting like a sink."

He'd lost me already.

"Okay."

"In New York, you turn the water on in the sink and—zip!—it goes right down the drain."

"Yes."

"In Mexico, we like to turn the water on and then we like to watch it go around and around," he motioned his hand like the pretend water swilling around the pretend sink, "until, finally, eventually, it goes down the drain."

I smiled.

"You understand?"

"Yes, I do, thank you."

"We're just different here, it's okay."

He Got Balls

A client called upset that his colleague got promotional stress balls and he didn't.

This incident led to about 36 hours of hilarious Job Notes:

"Omar called. Wants a set of balls. Salesman notified."

"Sales found some balls. Distro to be done."

"Shipped Omar his balls via FedEx."

"Omar expected to get some balls in the morning. Follow up."

"Omar has balls now and is very happy."

Honestly, if we could have stretched it out longer, we would have.

The Lucky Shirt

Midnight, phone rings.

"New York Customer Service."

"Hi, this is Jason Bell. I'm working on the RK2 deal."

Job was one of our active deals but not on the note.

"How can I help you?"

"I have a favor to ask."

"Okay."

"I'm in San Francisco and I have a big meeting tomorrow."

"Okay."

"This is gonna sound silly, but I have this shirt... well, it's kinda my lucky shirt."

"Okay."

"And I left it at my parents' house last weekend."

"Where do they live?"

"South Jersey."

"What time's your meeting?"

"3PM Pacific."

Look at the clock. Three hours down. Three, four hours back, that's 7AM. Six hour flight. Two hours max at airports. That's 3PM New York time, noon Pacific. An hour to get to the client. Throw an hour in for buffer.

"Man on board we can get it there by 2PM your time."

"Could you?"

"Yes. What's your parents' address?"

He gave us the address.

"Phone number."

He gave us his parents' phone number.

"Do they know we're coming?"

"I'll call them as soon as we hang up."

"Okay. The driver'll call when he's about fifteen minutes away. Where in San Francisco do you want the shirt delivered?"

He gave us another address.

"And your phone tomorrow?"

He gave another number.

"Okay, that's it."

"Really?"

"Really."

"You guys are amazing."

"Thank you, sir. And... good luck at your meeting."

Let's Get It On

The IPO's filed, we're just doing clean up now. The clients are waiting for the bookproof and this thing'll print tonight. A long week has just about come to an end.

BzzzBING!

I go to the room and open the door. Music's playing: Marvin Gaye's "Let's Get It On" is coming out of someone's laptop.

Some of the people in this room became millionaires today. An already-attacked tray of champagne flutes sits among the discarded markup, loose pages, and a small avalanche of old proofs on the table.

Clients are milling around the room, some are sway-dancing, some chatting, a few by the windows, looking at the city lights come up, drinking. If this were an apartment instead of a conference room, it might be a party. A laid-back, very business-attired party.

"Laura!" the attorney says. "Celebrate with us!"

"Oh, thanks," I say smiling, "but I'm still working."

"Come on," he says. I've worked a number of his deals these

last few years. "One quick dance." He grabs my hand and pulls me toward him. "Two minutes."

"Alright, one quick one." I put my hand on his shoulder and my palm in his other hand. He leads me down the border of the conference room, guiding my arm up for one or two spins in slow motion to the music.

It's a happy conference room. Happy clients.

The song winds its way down and I take my leave, adjourning back to the real world of rustling pages and paper cups.

"What are you smiling about?" my Team Leader asks back at my desk.

"Oh nothing…," I say, unlocking my screen. "This place has its moments."

I see him nod in my periphery.

"It certainly does."

Madrid

DAY 1

"So, what's the scene there?"

"It's a fucking nightmare," I say to my two colleagues over the phone. "The fax machine is the kind with the roll of paper you have to rip off. The fucking copy machine can only make thirty pages at a time. The proof's 160 pages and we've got ten clients coming in the morning. I need to order equipment."

I look out the window down on the streets of Madrid and take a drag of my smoke.

"Oh, fuck, that's bad," one says.

"Steve Spencer says order whatever you need." Steve Spencer's the salesperson.

"Okay, cool," I say. "How 'bout someone who speaks Spanish? These clients are gonna want food and stuff and all I can say is 'Necessito un recibo.'"

"Hahaaaa," Angel laughs.

"What's that mean?" my other colleague says.

"I need a receipt," Angel chirps.

We have a laugh.

"One nice thing though…," I say, readjusting the ashtray on my desk. "You can smoke in the office."

"Europeans, man, ya gotta love 'em."

DAY 2

On the phone again, ten hours into a week of 18-hour days.

"Dude, the colorwork is all fucked up. I'm in the conference room and the guy's lookin' at Cover 2 and he's like, 'This looks great... but how does it fold out?'"

"What??"

"Yeah, I'm like, 'fold out?' This job's supposed to be a fucking gatefold?"

"Not that I know of."

"Well, what else could it be? The guy is in there freaking folding the Epson in half to show me. It's a gatefold."

"I'll call BBC."

"Thanks. See if they can think up a way to get me new color-work by tomorrow, it's not like I have an Epson printer here."

"Yeah... Oh, by the way, we got you the Spanish speaker. Some chick from LA is working in London this summer. She'll be there tonight."

"Great, thanks."

"Now, let's discuss the most important thing: did you try the coffee? We heard it's like crack."

DAY 3

The little office I'm using is attached to the conference room. The banker in-house asks if he can use my spare desk and phone to make a call.

"Of course," I say. I'm working on the other side of the room but it's impossible not to overhear him.

"Anna? Hello, darling, it's Peter. God, I miss you. Listen, I'm in Madrid working and planning to head to the beach this weekend, you should join me! I've got an incredible place reserved... Oh, that's too bad, darling... Well, sorry darling, but listen, I've got to run, I'll call again soon, okay?"

He hangs up. Aw, so sad, I think, his girl can't make it for the weekend.

He dials again.

"Olivia? Hello, darling, it's Peter. God, I miss you." WHAT? "Listen, I'm in Madrid working and—"

Four calls in a row like this until he got a taker.

Fucking bankers.

DAY 4

Another 18-hour day in progress. The female accountant pokes her head in my door around 9PM.

"Can I bum a smoke?" she says.

"Sure." I nod to my pack on the edge of the table. She takes a cigarette, lights it, and hops up to sit on the desk by the window. I'm matching up some pages on the other side of the room.

"So, you know the guy from Bear? The tall one from London?" she says his name. It's the guy from yesterday.

"Of course," I say.

"What do you think of him?" she says, taking a drag of her smoke and blowing it out the window. She's a pretty blonde, maybe thirty.

"No comment," I say.

A minute or so passes.

"He's a bit of an asshole, isn't he?" she says.

I look in her direction and then back to my pages.

"No comment."

She laughs.

DAY 5

We finally wrap the in-house and the chick from LA and I sit on the tiny balcony of my hotel at 11PM eating crappy takeout and drinking a bottle of wine. We look down on the street lined with gorgeous fountains that glow in the dark.

"We never even got to see the city," she says.

In Madrid for a week and we've literally only been to the hotel and the office.

"Yeah," I say. "It's always like that."

DAY 6

I go to the concierge desk at the airport to pick up my ticket. The woman asks me for a confirmation number. I don't have one.

"Can I use your phone?" I say. I dial New York and get the salesman, Steve Spencer. He gives me the number.

"And, by the way, I upgraded you to First Class," he says.

"Wow, thanks, Steve," I say. I've never been in First Class.

When I settle into my seat, I think I smell something burning and ask the stewardess.

"Oh, that's the chocolate chip cookies baking," she says.

I wait for my cookie.

The flight is a pleasure. First Class all the way.

100 Clients In-House

Nightside, 9PM.

100 clients in-house.

I'm rushing down the hallway, my hands full of pages, Tom Junior careening toward me with four ice buckets sloshing water. I give him the eyeball and as we zip past, he says, "Global warming, who knew?"

Wish I'd written down every hilarious thing he's ever said.

I Don't Think This is the Lobby

"You ready?"

"Yep, just finished turning," I say, grabbing my coat. Nightside reps don't normally get to cut out for a sales outing but I worked a freebie job for this salesman and he's taking me out to dinner with the clients.

"Munzi's coming too," Hillerbrand says, as I check out with my manager. Mark Munzi surfaces from the 9th floor stairway and the three of us head down in the elevator. On the street, we squeeze into the backseat of a town car, my knees buckling up in the middle position.

"Uptown, East 60s," Hillerbrand directs the driver. We settle in for the ride.

"So where are we going for dinner?" I say.

"Well, we're not exactly going to dinner," Hillerbrand ends his sentence in a muffled laugh, as men of a certain age who know something you don't know are apt to do.

"Okay…," I say. I look at Munzi next to me.

"We're going to Guccione's," Munzi says.

"Guccione's?" I've never heard of Guccione's, not that I'm really in the loop with many Sales-caliber restaurants in Manhattan.

"Bob Guccione's," Hillerbrand says. "You know, the guy who owns Penthouse. He's having a party."

"What??" I say. "Are you kidding?"

"Woolery might be there," Munzi says, across to Hillerbrand. Munzi has a client whose defining trait (for us, anyway) is that he's Chuck Woolery's cousin. It's a small world, people, and now you are all three degrees of separation from Chuck Woolery.

"Are we really going to a party at Bob Guccione's? Because I'm totally not dressed for that," I say. I'm in a business suit, and while it might be fine for a man to arrive at a party at Bob Guccione's in a business suit, I have a feeling the ladies may be dressed somewhat differently.

"Yes, we are. And you look fine," Hillerbrand says.

Thus began the longest cab ride of my life. I don't like to be unprepared for things and this was pretty much as unprepared as I could conceive of at 25 years old: not being in the right outfit for the evening's event.

We pulled up to a tremendous townhouse on East 67th and hustled up the stairs. When the huge door sucked closed behind us we looked around. The place was insane: marble and gold leaf everywhere.

"I don't think this is the lobby," Munzi said with a laugh. It was not the lobby.

We merged into the crowd. The townhouse was incredibly furnished, with stunning artwork everywhere. And not just any art—the guy had original Picassos hanging on the walls.

An hour later I was loitering with my drink in a hallway when Munzi came by.

"Have you been to the bathroom yet?" he said.

"No…"

"There's a toilet in there made of SOLID GOLD. A solid gold toilet!"

Hillerbrand bumped me on the elbow.

"This is why no one wants to work at Bowne of Oklahoma City," he said. "It doesn't get better than New York."

Another hour later we were on the lower level, I'd call it a basement but it was like no basement I'd ever seen. An inground pool stretched the length of the footprint, with a small room at its end where people were mingling at the bar. A security guard stood by the wall between the two areas.

"Glass of Pinot Grigio," I said, leaning into the bartender.

"What is all that stuff?" Munzi waved toward the pool where there were numerous bizarre objects suspended from the walls and ceiling.

I shrugged and took a sip of my wine.

"Wow, that's good," I said to the bartender.

"Six hundred and fifty dollars a bottle, it better be good," he said back to me.

"I'm gonna go ask the guard what that stuff is," Munzi said.

Hillerbrand leaned in. "Can you believe this place?"

"It's unbelievable," I said, looking out the set of glass doors leading to a back courtyard.

Munzi returned and hunched between us.

"It's the set props from Caligula!" Munzi announced.

"Oh my god."

The whole night was surreal.

At 11PM we squeezed around a table at The Palm with a couple of other people from the party, ordered more drinks and stuffed our heads with obscene amounts of food.

Two bars and three hours after that I was in a town car heading home on Route 3 in New Jersey.

"Pull over," I slurred to the driver as he flew over the Hackensack River Bridge. And my night revisited me in reverse.

You Got a Light?

When it's slow in the summertime, I meet Will in the client lounge and we sit by the windows on upholstered armchairs to have our smoke and our meandering conversation.

In the early days, down to the loading dock with Doretha if it wasn't too cold.

The nightly with Tino at 11:30PM, a pre-turn ritual bonding our two shifts together, where we hash all the dirt that's not part of the turn.

Chain smoking the wee hours of the nights away at an outdoor table on Spring Street with the guys from my team.

And that last one with Stu, the day before he died, in front of the building while people spun in and out of the revolving door behind us. When I heard he passed all I could think was, "But I just had a smoke with him yesterday…"

Please Scan

"So you know how the guy is in a fight with his design firm ever since that Bella Modella..." Heather shuffled the job bag and swiveled toward me in her chair. "...Let's call it that Bella Modella *incident?*"

The famous model apparently did not appreciate her likeness appearing in the 8-page gatefold of the IPO for a company whose claim to fame was that they made the embellishments used to decorate the undergarments of a popular clothing label. Her attorney had sent a cease and desist, leaving two obvious holes in the colorwork spread.

"Yeah," I said.

"Well, this is what he sent to replace Miss Bella's photos."

A square box sat on the counter for our turnover.

"Jeez, how many photos did he send? We only need two..." I started opening the flap.

"Oh, it's not photos." Heather looked away dismissively. I looked at Heather. Looked at the box. Was this going to be like the movie Seven? What's in the box, Heather?!

I peeled open the flap. The second flap. I looked back at Heather, who was trying not to laugh. The next flap.

"Oh my god." I started laughing when I saw the contents. I reached in, and lifted out a pair of red underwear with one finger. "Is he kidding?"

"Please scan," she said handing me the client memo that had accompanied the box.

We collapsed in a fit of giggles.

"Please scan?" I repeated, a little too loudly.

"I'd like to see their faces at BBC if we sent this over!!" she said.

We couldn't stop laughing. People were starting to look in our direction.

She picked another item from the box and held it up, a black lacy bra.

"Please scan!" we said in unison.

We were cracking up.

A salesman heading down to the 9th floor did a double take and kept walking.

"This is hilarious!" I said. "What did you tell him?"

"Oh, it just came in 15 minutes ago, that phone call's all yours, baby." Heather took the job bag off her desk and set it next to the box.

"Oh, god," I said, still laughing.

"You'll know how to put it to him *delicately*," she said.

"Sir, yes, we got the package. The thing is, sir, we can only scan things that are flat, like a photo or a print..."

He reminded me of the issue he was having with the design firm; they wouldn't give him any of that stuff.

"Right, sir, but we can only scan things that are images..."

I rolled back from my desk.

"…I know, sir, and we want to help, but it has to be something flat."

He wouldn't give up. I stood up at my desk now, physically willing this call to end.

"Sir, I'm sorry, but... we can't scan underwear."

A rep walking by gave me the crazy eyeballs like WHAT AND WHO ARE YOU TALKING TO? I pulled one pair of underwear out of the box and he folded in half laughing.

A few days later I came in for the afternoon turnover and another package had arrived from the client. It was flat alright. A long, flat rectangle. But the thing was huge. Still wrapped in brown paper, leaning against the CS counter, it took up about three-quarters length of the counter. The thing must have been ten feet long and maybe three or four feet high.

Now what?

We peeled back the paper across the front to reveal it. A woman's head, body, a woman in underwear laying down... Oh my god, it had dirt on it. What is this?

It was the billboard from the side of a bus. A used billboard.

The accompanying memo: "Please scan."

We couldn't scan that either.

Paris

There's nothing funny to say about Paris. My weeks there were tortured, riddled by insomnia, and consumed with negative effects for my personal life that followed me all the way back to New York.

There were bright spots, of course:

Arrival.

Departure.

And the breakfast ham.

The breakfast ham in Paris was excellent.

I Should've Been a Teacher

He arrived on a Monday evening, a young attorney with dark hair and a fresh face and a duffle bag packed like he was coming to a sleepover.

By Tuesday night he realized his mistake. In his second change of clothes he asked if we might have a room for him to sleep.

"Maybe around 2AM," I told him. "Before then, you can try the lounge."

Wednesday was especially rough, pages turning all day, his group had grown to close to thirty, stuffed into the two conference rooms we'd selected for their Monday group-size, and spilling into a third for proofreaders and phone calls. They ran edits through the night.

When he came to the counter on Thursday afternoon, he was wearing a t-shirt. I supposed the duffle bag had run dry.

"Laura, you've gotta get me out of this room. I can't work in there, it's too crowded." The bankers had arrived, hoarding table space and talking on their cellphones. They'd brought their own attorneys, and this guy wasn't getting along with any of them.

"I'm sorry, we don't have any more rooms open," I said.

"There's got to be something. It's an issue of personalities. I can't work in that room," he said.

"I'm sorry, we're completely full right now. But something will probably open up after midnight."

"What about there?" he said, looking behind me to an empty desk about ten feet from my own inside the Customer Service Department. The desk was off to the side of our team, normally occupied by a dayside support person. But this was nights, no one sat there.

"I'm sorry, sir, we can't have you in the department. We have other confidential documents working in here."

"But it's out of the way," he insisted, "And, look," he pointed, "it's right by the door. I understand about the confidentiality, I could go right to it, I wouldn't see anything."

"Sir, it's really not our policy, I'm sorry."

"Laura, please. You know me..." He put his arms on the counter. "I can't go back to that conference room."

I didn't know him, but after four days of a non-stop in-house, you develop an oddly personal relationship with certain clients. He was just a regular guy, stuck. He was wearing a t-shirt for god's sake. We weren't friends or anything, but he was my main attorney and when I looked in his face across the counter I could see what it was and I felt bad for him. He was desperate. This week was nothing like he'd expected it to be. I thought of the duffle bag.

"Please," he said again.

"Lemme talk to my manager," I said.

Thirty minutes later the client was sitting at his new desk, practically beside us INSIDE THE CUSTOMER SERVICE

DEPARTMENT. It had been like moving day, the client setting up his laptop and making several trips to bring in all his papers and proofs, and, of course, his duffle bag. My colleague and I stared at each other uncomfortably across our median. It was completely unsettling.

"This is fucked up," my colleague mouthed in slow motion, eyeballs wild. It was. It was not the natural order of things. A client inside Customer Service: it was disturbing. Truly disturbing now that we were doing it.

A few hours later the client signaled me. He had kept to his promise, not venturing outside his designated area and the strict pathway to the door. He'd only been there a few hours and had agreed to go back to the conference room by the morning, but we had to be so guarded with him there, it felt like he'd been there all week.

I approached his desk.

"Do you wanna have dinner with me?" he whispered.

That was not what I was expecting.

"When?" I said.

"Right now."

I looked around, maybe to confirm that, yes, we were still in the Customer Service Department. Xeroxes going, phones ringing, reps walking around. Yep, we were still here.

"I'm working," I said.

"No, in the lounge, they have dinner out." He really didn't get this place, did he? There's a class structure, and clients are at the top.

"That's just for clients. Customer Service doesn't eat off the buffet," I said. That wasn't exactly true; we sneak the scraps around 10PM, or an irresistible shrimp when we're passing by, and, alright, once in a while someone might put a lobster tail in their pocket, or wrap the fax they're holding around a cannoli and then eat said cannoli in the hallway, but as far as this conversation was concerned, the correct answer was no, we do not eat off the client buffet. And definitely not with a client in the middle of the shift.

"You don't? Well, can I at least bring you back something? You saved my life here."

"No, no, please don't do that, it's okay," I said. A client bringing a Customer Service Rep food from the client buffet? That was just crazy talk. This guy was losing it.

"Alright," he said, a little dejected. This was such a bad idea, letting a client in here. All the boundaries were getting skewed.

He sat back from his work, exhausted.

"You know...," he said, "I should've been a teacher."

We stared at each other for a few seconds while that hung in the air. This client was beaten; he wasn't cut out for this. No one brings a duffle bag.

I thought of that other dimension: the one with him in khakis at a blackboard, sun coming through the windows, the one where he leans over in the middle of a classroom and helps a kid with some problem. The one where he grabs his keys from his desk at 4PM and heads home.

I could see it. Just for a second, it was almost real, somewhere.

"It's okay," I said quietly. "You're gonna file this document tomorrow, and then we're gonna print it, and then you can do whatever you want."

He looked at me. God, he looked so much older than he did on Monday.

"Right," he came back to earth. "You're right. Thanks."

I went to my desk and when I glanced over to check on him, he was back in his papers.

Pool Sharks

We're running the pool table at a West Village bar in our business suits at 3AM on a Wednesday.

I take a drag of my smoke and balance it on the edge of the pool table, burning tip out. Knock the last ball in.

"C'mon…," one of the NYU boys says as he shuffles his way back around the table to return his stick.

Courtney hops off a stool and clinks her beer to mine. I take a swig. She squats down and pulls the triangle out to rack another game.

"A for Effort, kids," she says over her shoulder. "Who's next?"

Knicks Game

We'd gone crazy looking for it. The package my client swore his office sent us and was signed for. All his markup was in there.

The client had arrived in house and immediately requested the package his office had forwarded.

We couldn't find it.

He had a signature, but it had come in right around the afternoon shift turnover and the person who supposedly signed for it was gone.

Back and forth I went: from the conference room, to Shipping, back to the conference room, back to Shipping, telling my manager, back to the conference room—the client getting increasingly frustrated—back to my desk, calling the salesperson, checking all the other teams in Customer Service, back to check Shipping again, back to the conference room where the client was now in a state.

We never lose things. This package was lost. Lost! It was practically unspeakable.

We didn't have it. We couldn't find it. We couldn't replicate it.

And we couldn't replace it.

I apologized to the client and told him the search was over.

"So, you're telling me," his words were coming out too slow, this guy was going to blow up. "I'm going to have to do ALL THAT WORK again because you can't find it?"

He was furious.

"I'm sorry, sir."

"I can't fucking believe this!"

The guy had a right to be pissed, his whole original markup was gone. It was at least hours, possibly days or weeks, worth of work he'd have to recreate. Not to mention we're talking about confidential documents that have not yet been released to the public.

He sat down at the conference room table and looked like he was trying to regroup. I left the room feeling pretty beaten.

By this point I'd seen clients in all sorts of frustration. It's never comfortable, but it's the nature of the business. These guys are stressed. They're sleep-deprived. They're under strict deadlines. And a lot of them are assholes.

The year before I'd worked a deal where the two main attorneys from opposing firms hated each other. Their weeks in-house escalated from arguments to heated arguments. Then there was a brief physical altercation in the room. For a week they'd worked in separate conference rooms, the presence of the other was so intolerable.

Finally on the day of the filing there was an all-out sanity breakdown when one attorney picked up a conference room chair and threw it across the table at the other. A complete racket ensued, the other members of the working group backing away to the walls.

I'd exited the room, closed the door behind me, and called the salesman from the hallway phone.

"You've gotta get up here right now. They're throwing chairs."

I don't know what the salesman did when he went in that room (RIP Stu Banfield), but the noise stopped and that job fucking filed. Just barely—Stu and I sprinting down the hallway —but it fucking filed on time.

So, that day I knew this angry client and his lost package wasn't going to be anything like that.

But how could this happen? We never lose things.

About 30 minutes later, the client called me back to the conference room. He was significantly less angry.

"You know what would make me feel better about this situation?" he said.

"What?"

"Tickets to tonight's Knicks game."

Oh, now I see.

All that running around was for this bullshit setup.

"You know, if you ever want tickets to a game," I said, "all you have to do is ask."

"Okay."

"Okay," I said back to him. I stood there waiting. We could be assholes, too, see.

"I'd like tickets to tonight's Knicks game," he said finally.

"No problem. Two or four?"

"Two."

Without another word, he opened his briefcase and pulled out the "lost" package. Did he pick it up from reception? Have it with him the whole time? I don't know. He undid the rubber-band around his markup. Handed the pages to me.

I left the room. Called the salesman and told him we had the markup and needed the Knicks tickets.

At least the client will be out of here early, I thought, aggressively bumping the pages 1, 2, 3, 4 for typesetting.

"Fuckin' bastard," I muttered, stamping 5, 6, 7, and on.

We never lose anything.

Disconcerting

I was in the conference room. It was a Colombian issuer, and the company and their attorneys had flown in from South America to get the deal done.

The in-house was going fine, and I had just finished my very short speech regarding the print turnaround and their cutoff times to get books to various locations. The clients from the company conferred with their attorneys in Spanish afterward. I had no idea what they were saying.

"We have one question," the guy from the company said after their huddle.

"Okay," I nodded.

"Are you a Mexican?" he said.

I smiled. Huh?

"I asked you a simple question. Are you a Mexican or not?"

He was serious. I straightened my face. "I am not, why?"

His colleague and the attorneys all stared at me.

"Because Mexicans make promises they can't keep." The other guy from the company nodded in agreement as if this was a well-known fact.

Truly bewildered, I collected myself.

"If you clear to print by noon tomorrow, you *will* have books on Friday. And… I'm Italian," I inexplicably felt the need to add.

They looked at each other and conferred again in Spanish across the corner of the table. One of the attorneys ended their dialogue, saying "It's okay, s'okay."

"Very well," the client from the company said. He clasped his hands on the table and looked up at me.

"Thank you, that is all," he said.

Morgan Stanley Blue

"So we're at this bar in Alphabet City…" I interrupt myself and turn to Dean. "Wait, was it Saint Patrick's Day?"

"No."

"Was it?"

"Wait, I think it was…" He considers as he takes a swig of his beer. "No, it wasn't. Sam took us there, remember?" Sam is my British team leader.

Dean explains to the group. "Sam dragged us to this bar where everyone in the place was Irish or British. It was like we stepped into an alternate universe…" He looks at me. "Maybe it WAS Saint Patrick's Day…"

We're huddled into a lopsided circle at the bar of one of our usual haunts at 2:30AM on a Monday. The life of the nightside Customer Service Rep basically involves going to work and then going out drinking with people from work and talking about work.

"Anyway," I continue, "there's this girl at the bar Dean is trying to get with, this Irish girl and—"

"C'mon, I was just being friendly." Dean says.

I roll my eyes. "Yeah, okay."

Back to the group I continue. "And the girl is bombed, she's wearing this outfit that's like a brown sweater that's a tiny skirt except it's beige from her tits up and she's going around to all the guys saying, 'Drink me up! I'm a pint of Guinness!'"

"It was a very nice sweater," Dean says.

The group chuckles.

"So Dean starts talking to the girl, and then the girl says—all slow like—she's like, 'Do you want to feel my screeeew?'"

The group responds with eyebrows, like whatthefuck does that even mean? Do you want to feel my screw?

"Right, so of course Dean has no idea what it means either but of course he's like, 'HELL, YEAH!'" Everyone laughs. I take a drag of my smoke.

"And then the girl reaches down underneath her skirt..." Dean hangs his head as I finish the story. "And pulls off her leg! THE GIRL HAD A PEG LEG!"

We're all cracking up.

"That's fucking crazy," someone says.

"Moral of the story: stay on the west side," Dean says. We all drink to that.

"Oh, and the Morgan Stanley thing," Dean says.

"Oh yeah," I pick up. "So at this same bar, I'm talking to this guy and it turns out he works for Morgan Stanley... And Dean comes by, TOTALLY interrupting us..."

"Yeah, that's right, Laura was about to embark on a deep meaningful relationship with this guy," Dean says.

We all laugh. I backhand Dean on the chest.

"Anyway, I introduce the guy to Dean and say he works for Morgan Stanley. Hey, we all have something in common, right?"

That settles in while I take another drag of my smoke.

"And Dean just looks at the guy and says, 'Morgan Stanley? Did you say Morgan Stanley?'" I flick my ashes into the bar ashtray.

"And the guy's like, 'Yeah, I work for Morgan Stanley.' And Dean gets right up to his face and says, 'Yoooouuuuuu!'—like he's the fucking witch from *The Wizard of Oz*—he goes, 'Yoouuuu! Youuuu and your FUCKING BLUE, MAN!'"

We're hysterical; a joke only a financial printer would get. All Morgan Stanley finals print in their signature blue, a requirement that means you have to wash down the press before you can print another job.

"The guy was like, 'What the fuck?'"

Our laughter winds down and someone else starts the next tale. I grab my beer off the bar and Joey T squeezes in beside me to signal the bartender for another round.

"Great story," he says, clicking his beer to mine.

I love these guys.

On Overtime

"New York Customer Service, this is Laura."

"What?"

I've been working so much I answer the phone in my apartment as if I'm at the office.

Thanksgiving

It was Thanksgiving Day and I was in the office because a deal I was working on was coming in-house: clients descending on our offices to work their document in real-time.

"Did you tell them it's Thanksgiving??" my mom had wanted to know.

Thanksgiving was the latest in Financial Print Customer Service expectations my mother did not understand.

"They know it's Thanksgiving, Mom."

This deal had been cranking on relentlessly for months. An Argentinian merger, the document was a monster, pushing 400 pages of financials and another 300 of text. Let's not even discuss the exhibits, which we kept in quarantined stacks protected by a police line of "DO NOT TOUCH" signs drawn by the third shift rep.

This was the late '90s and international registrations had not yet been phased into the SEC's electronic system, which meant this job was also a paper filing. Just making copies for the conference room was an ordeal, forget it—running the filing package took half a shift and two guys plus the client to carry it on the flight to DC. We were up to Amendment 4.

The clients banged the shit out of this document. The guy who turned over to me would start the turnover by breaking into the chorus of "Don't Cry For Me Argentina"—and my night pretty much went downhill from there.

PDF edits were unheard of at this time. The company in Argentina would fax changes and instructions for hours on end, sometimes in Spanish, which we would have to translate to English before committing to the document. I'd wait for the fax cover page to inch its way out and see the death knell notation, "Fax 1 of 3, 171 pages follow," the 1's all written with a South American hook on their heads. I'd pull off some pages to process and then try not to kill myself when our fax guy, Charlie, called me at my desk: "My dear, your Buenos Aires #1 started coming in crooked at page 156, #2 skipped from page 20 to 43, tell them to re-send, okay?"

Markup cut off all around the edge of the page, I'd spend an hour doing tedious language-barriered copy clarification with Argentina, and then field 30 calls from the typesetting site after I sent them the changes.

And then a messenger would arrive with a five-pound Redweld of the New York edits.

The deal was all-encompassing; I started having dreams about it. In the worst, a repetitive one, I was receiving a 400-page fax from Argentina on three different colored papers with the markup referencing pages on other colors. I'd have Sisyphus-style dreams about hauling proofs into the conference room. Dreams about the handwriting of the woman who worked in our Buenos Aires office. Dreams about bumping up the filing package and realizing around folio F-326 that I had somehow skipped a page. Seriously, I should have sought mental health counseling from working on this deal.

The main attorney was a guy named Mike Terger, a New Yorker short in stature but tall in demands. He was early-30s, with a stocky build and the tiny hopeful gleam of future partnership in one eye. He was a tough client, not because he was particularly mean-spirited or particularly unreasonable, but because the combination of his ambition and the enormity of his document made every directive a time-consuming pain in the ass. He had a lot of directives. By month three, I'd reached a point of resigned misery every time a colleague said, "Laur, you got Mike Terger holding on 8-0." I swear this guy was holding on 8-0 every freaking time I walked by my desk.

That said, the attorney's job was much harder than mine, so I had no animosity about it. Guy probably worked twenty hours a day and, if his document's Amendment 4 was any indication, there was no end in sight. That, however, didn't stop me from repeatedly saying, "I fucking hate everybody," to my Team Leader, who would usually respond, "You've got Mike Terger holding again on 8-0."

When they came in-house that Thanksgiving Day, I was the only one in the office. I was greeting Mike Terger and two of his henchmen at the counter when the CS phone rang. The first clients had just arrived, Mike Terger still wearing his business-black winter coat and grey scarf at the counter, taking off his gloves as we discussed the game plan for the day. His two colleagues were behind him, in their own business-black coats and grey scarves, associates in their 20s, just a few years older than me.

It was already the early afternoon of Thanksgiving and it was clear none of us wanted to be there.

Reception was off for the day, so all the calls were bouncing into CS. I excused myself to answer the phone, just ten feet away from the counter near Team B. It was for Mike.

"It's for you, you want me to transfer it into the conference room?" The whole of CS was empty, just me and the three attorneys standing at the counter.

"No, put them on speaker," he said, already making this day as annoying as possible.

"Okay." I put it on speaker and turned it up.

"Mike Terger," he said.

A high-pitched female voice emerged from the Team B speaker. "Michael, this is your mother. Dinner will be served at six o'clock whether you're here or not!"

"Hold on, Mom," he said. I pushed the button to put the call on hold, trying to hide my smile. The two associates were in a similar state.

"Put it into the conference room, Laura."

Yeah, okay.

That phone call made the whole deal worth it. And we did get out of there before six.

Epilogue:

Some time later, Mike Terger announced he was leaving his firm. It was a bit unorthodox, but I made him a card. For the cover of the card I created a collage of the messiest, most jacked up markup they'd sent in over the months on this deal. Shrunken pages, angled together and overlapping each other, filled with their crazy handwriting, arrows pointing to riders looping around paragraphs, new sentences squashed long-ways in the margins, pages where they had suddenly decided to change every third word in the document—the whole collage scaled down to fit one side of a simple 8.5 x 11 folded card stock; I dummied it up on the office copy machine. On the inside I wrote, "Best wishes in your next endeavors! We'll miss you!!" The three shifts of CS Reps who worked on the deal and the salesperson signed it. He thought it was hilarious. Until he realized it was his own markup.

Paper Clips

"But, listen, here's the thing," I say to the completely disinterested third shift rep about the in-house I'm turning. "Every batch of pages you bring in there they want them paper clipped to each page of the original markup."

"I'm not fuckin' doin' that," he says.

"Dude, I'm telling you, that's the way they want it."

"I'm not doin' it. You run your shift your way, I've got the next eight hours, alright?" He grabs the pages due back for the room off the counter where we're turning and heads off to the conference room. These fucking guys, fine, whatever, you got the next eight.

I start cleaning up my shit, getting ready to leave. Ninety seconds later the rep returns.

"Where's that box of paper clips?" he says.

Yeah, thought so.

Front Cover

The banker had submitted four rounds of changes to the spacing at the bottom of the prospectus cover where the underwriter names appear. His bank was co-underwriting the deal, and the standard is all underwriters with a common stake have their company names appear in the same point size on the cover. BigBank had been making repeated changes to the kerning (the spaces between characters) and remained unsatisfied with the cover's appearance.

I brought the fifth revision into the room and stood between BigBank and the other co-underwriter to review the page. They were already an hour past their deadline to get books on the street for tomorrow.

I held up the page with two hands and the two bankers looked over my shoulders.

"It's fine," the co-underwriter said.

"Nope, still no good," BigBank announced.

"Jesus H," an attorney sitting at the table said, putting his head in his hands.

"Sir, maybe I can help you better if you tell me exactly what the problem is," I said.

"The problem is...," BigBank thumbed at the co-underwriter, "their name looks longer than ours."

I glanced up at the co-underwriter, a tall lanky guy from Donaldson, Lufkin & Jenrette. The corner of his mouth turned up in the slightest.

Eyes on the page, I leaned toward the BigBank banker and quietly, as if an aside, said, "Sir, their name *is* longer than yours."

We three stared at the page again.

A few seconds passed as we all took in the reality of the number of characters in "BigBank" sitting beside "Donaldson, Lufkin & Jenrette" in exactly the same point size.

The DLJ guy shifted his weight.

The room waited.

"Alright," BigBank said, "I guess you can leave it."

A Night at the Printer's

By now I'm a Team Leader.

conference room

on the deal

the salesman's

I knew that the job

he said.

"Why?"

"Alright then."

"Okay

and the room

the pages

the client

unbelievable.

True story.

He Wasn't New York

You could tell he wasn't New York by the way he spoke: slower, more measured, choosing his words carefully. He didn't have a New York accent but he worked really hard at not having an Alabama one, and that counts for something.

The Ear

We're at a back table in The Ear performing our 1AM nightly ritual of drinking and commiserating on the topics of the day, namely: shitty dayside turnovers, composition fuck-ups, and jobs gone wrong. When a story starts, "I had a job that cleared to print…," you're in for a three drink minimum. Oh, let's face it, three drinks is the minimum regardless.

We love this place. Two blocks from the office, with its sloping floor and late-night kitchen, its paper tablecloths and glasses filled with crayons, its wooden beams and cramped beverage consumption, and its odd James Gandolfini sighting, this tiny joint is a historical landmark that at one time sat on the shoreline of the Hudson River, before urban development and the West Side Highway filled in blocks toward New Jersey.

There's a huge sculptured ear on a wall wedged beside a round table where we like to say, "Between you, me, and the ear," before spilling some company gossip.

But we're not at that table tonight.

We're between war stories when a guy around thirty wearing a shirt and tie approaches our table. "You guys from Bowne?" he says.

One of my colleagues slides his chair back across the warped planks to turn around and look up at him.

"Yeah, why?"

"I'm with Merrill," he gestured behind him to a gang sitting at a table a few feet away. One of the guys raised his beer to us. "We heard you talking and we're like, 'This is the same shit we're bitchin' about!'"

We all laugh. Merrill's another financial printer just a few blocks away.

"We're like, 'These guys must be from Bowne.'"

"Yeah, it's the same shit everywhere, right?" one of my group said.

"Chris Murphy," the spokesman introduced himself, holding out his hand for a shake with the guy sitting closest to him. We did a quick round of name exchange.

"You guys ever go down to Walker's?" he said.

"Sure."

"We'll see ya around then."

"See ya around," we said.

He headed back to his group.

"Too funny," my colleague said, adjusting his chair and then taking a swig of his beer.

We did see Chris Murphy around. We saw him around a lot once we knew to be looking for him. He ended up introducing me to my future husband.

Got Time?

Her phone rings.

"Kitchen," she answers.

"Got time?" I say.

"Come on back, baby."

I head out of Customer Service, through Shipping, past the freight elevator, and swipe my ID on the electronic lock in the Xerox Department to open the door that leads to the kitchen and client lounge. The sun's going down as it always is for this first smoke of the evening and my heels click on the tile as I see the panoramic of New Jersey stretch out behind the Hudson River past the client lounge. The glow of the sunset is sometimes red, sometimes orange, sometimes blue. Tonight's a blue night. I love when the city is held in blue. In another hour it'll be black, lights twinkling.

I meet her at the door to the ladies room in a hallway that runs behind the kitchen and is technically part of the client area but is virtually impossible for a client to find. How much money did the company spend, building this client bathroom whose sole purpose is employee smoke breaks and the odd saleswoman intrusion?

Who cares.

This is how friendships are made. In 10-minute increments over the course of years we discuss the issues of the day: our moods, life, love, sex, money, inconsequential dramas, perceived workplace injustices, and the unending daily minutiae of incidents at the Greenwich Street parking lot or where to buy a dildo in the West Village. Our cars, pets, apartment quandaries, colleagues, sneakers. We laugh, bitch, moan, once in a while we cry, and sometimes we just have a smoke.

We have our spots. She sits on the sink and listens to my current travesty, chiming in at the right time with an

"Mmm"

or

"Fuckin' ass"

or

"You're kidding"

or, with a pause between swipes of mascara,

"Is he just totally incompetent?"

I stand, readjust my clothes in the full length, reset my brain for the next two hours.

Sometimes our rant grows so lengthy that one or the other of us sets a new expectation: "I'm having two." And we continue.

We are passionate; we are young. Sometimes we are so fucking pissed our anger fills the room and reverberates off the tile, left to dissipate after our departure. We leave it all in the sanctuary.

She reapplies her makeup, blonde hair tight in a bun, face inches from the mirror, eyes squinting. She searches for something in her bag, cigarette hanging from her lips.

I check my pockets, over and over as if something new will appear there. We lower our voices and sometimes run to the stalls when we hear approaching footsteps.

It's a respite of sorts, these in-between moments, after the 5:30 filing deadline and before the next thing. Before she has to set up dinner.

When we're done, we go back to our posts, the door swinging closed behind us.

"See ya on the next."

"On the next, chickie."

People I Like

"All your clients are so nice," I say to the salesman hovering by our team. "How is it you don't have any clients that are... how should I put this..."

"Batshit crazy?" my teammate says.

"Narcissistic assholes?" another chimes in.

"Sadistic dickheads?" a third contributes.

The veteran chuckles.

"I'll tell you guys, a long time ago I decided something, and I've stuck with it and it's served me well," he says.

"What's that?" I say.

"I only sell to people I like."

My Pages on Carolina Ten

The room is ringing again. Fuck. I know what they're looking for —their pages. And I don't have 'em.

I go to the conference room for another uncomfortable conversation; there's only so long you can say things will be ready "shortly." These guys wanna know exactly how much longer. Five minutes? 12? 15? They're setting their watches to it.

They're New York attorneys but the job's a split with a Houston salesperson and so the pages are working in Dallas instead of Phoenix, our regular typesetting site. And, yeah, there's a difference.

New York attorneys expect pages back in 20 minutes, maybe 30. I've got pages with just a comma going in that have been hanging open for over an hour. The room is freaking out. I'm freaking out too! Back at my desk, I call Dallas.

"Hey, yeah, it's Laura in New York, I'm lookin' for my pages on Carolina Ten," I say into the phone at a hundred miles an hour.

"You got that lady up in New York City again," the guy drawls to his colleague, unsuccessfully muffling his receiver.

Someone else picks up.

"What job you lookin' for, darlin'?"

"Carolina Ten!" I say again, how fucking slow are these guys? "I've got cornermarks 16 to 30 been out for over an hour."

"Hold on a second," he says.

I'm standing at my counter with my phone cord wrapped around my hips, looking through my client's markup for the fifth time this hour. Fuck, these changes are nothing, Phoenix could've set new these pages in how long I'm waiting for these fucking changes.

"Gonna be another 15 or 20 minutes, maybe 30," the guy says. My head is about to explode.

"Are you kidding me??"

"You got a problem with it, call Houston."

Oh, I will fucking call Houston. You bet I'm gonna fucking call Houston.

I call Houston.

"This is Laura in New York, I need to speak to whoever's workin' Carolina Ten," I say when their Customer Service Department picks up.

A kid I've never heard of answers the phone.

"Listen," I tell him, "I know you set this job up in Dallas, but I've gotta move it to Phoenix, we're just not getting the turnaround we need."

"Well…," he says slowly, "Carolina Ten is supposed to work in Dallas."

"I get that," I say, "But I'm tellin' you I've got 15 cornermarks of light AA's been out for over an hour and the clients are freaking out."

BzzzBING! My room is ringing again. Fucking great.

"Salesman says it works in Dallas," he says.

"Well, I've got a NEW YORK salesman and a room full of NEW YORK clients and we're only up to cornermark 30 and Dallas can't fucking turn the shit around!"

"There's no reason to curse at me, ma'am," he says.

I see my conference room number still lit on the board like a dagger.

"I've gotta go, the room is ringing again wondering where their freaking pages are."

Back at the conference room, two of the clients are now in the hallway plotting my demise. Back to check my printer to see if any pages have miraculously appeared. They haven't.

I call Dallas again.

"This is Laura in New York, I'm lookin' for my pages on Carolina Ten," I say for the dozenth time today.

"Almost done, we're just finishing the compsupe," he says.

"WHAT? Why are you compsuping the job? This is an in-house, it's running unpaginated," I say.

"Listen, lady, we work this account all the time and it... runs... paginated," the guy says.

I've got eight attorneys marking up the proof, every page of which will now have a different serial number than the master Dallas is running out. My main attorney is gonna have a fucking conniption when he sees his page doesn't slug ex-fucking-actly.

"How far did it run?" I say, consulting my own master, which is now basically garbage.

"PN 64," he says.

"Alright."

I call Houston.

"Did you know they're running this job paginated in Dallas?" I ask him.

"Um, lemme check," he says.

"Either you know or you don't," I say. "In-houses run unpaginated. The clients are still marking up the document and now I'm gonna have to hand-mark all the PN numbers on this thing." I'm just venting now. "And I STILL don't have any pages to bring back to the room! Pages are out for 75 minutes and Dallas is tellin' me it could be another half hour! This job has GOT to move."

"Hold on a second…"

When he picks up again he says, "I'm being told this account typically has a page turn of at least an hour. It's not a problem."

"Not a problem? This is an in-house! The attorneys are—wait, whaddaya mean you're 'being told'?"

I hear a sound, a crinkling in the receiver.

"Are you workin' this job OR NOT?" I say.

More sounds, a muffling… is he crying?

"ARE YOU WORKIN' THIS JOB OR NOT??" I say again, fairly unhinged.

"It's my first day, ma'am."

Jesus Christ. He's definitely crying.

I pause, but find I have no empathy reserves tonight, sorry.

"Well… you know what they say, don'tcha?"

"What's that, ma'am?"

"THERE'S NO CRYING IN FINANCIAL PRINT!" I shout, channeling my inner Tom Hanks.

I'm done. I cut a renegade work order for Phoenix. The pages from Dallas finally start eeking out of my printer. When the clients submit the next batch of changes, I send them to Phoenix. All the pages go to Phoenix now, the site that knows when I ask where my fucking pages are the next thing I want to hear is an *exact* time or pages coming out of my device. The site where I can fax them 20 pages of markup and by the time cornermark 18 is spooling through, cornermarks 1-5 are coming out of my goddamn printer. Problem solved.

Houston calls a few hours later. The job is in Phoenix now, I've calmed down and so have the clients.

"They done for the night?" the kid in Houston wants to know.

"No, they're still here," I say.

"Dallas says they haven't gotten pages in a while," he says.

"Yeah, well, I moved the job to Phoenix," I say.

"You… can't do that."

"I've already done it, it's done."

"Hold on a second," he says.

I swivel my chair back and forth while I wait. I'll definitely be in the Director's office tomorrow over this job. Frank will steeple his hands together and I'll stare at his hairy knuckles while he gives me the what-for, but tonight? Tonight I only hear the lovely whirl of my printer as my beautiful pages from Phoenix churn out onto the device.

Intercom 2

It's 11PM when the overhead emits a click—someone's connected but hasn't said anything yet. A faint music starts coming through, a familiar tune, I can't exactly place it though… I look at my team. Maybe five seconds in it hangs up.

"Was that *The Facts of Life* theme song?" the guy across from me asks.

I laugh.

"It totally was!" I say.

He sings a line or two under his breath as he gets back to his in-house.

The overhead clicks in again.

"Jo Polniaczek, please call the operator. Jo Polniaczek, please call the operator."

Just one of the indescribable moments gone forever, as we all crack up and get back to work.

The Autistic

"There's gotta be a better way to do this," my colleague says. He's holding a pair of scissors, surrounded by small piles of labels that have been cut from the sheets provided by an underwriter.

"Yeah, breakin' down labels sucks," I say. The underwriters send in sheets of labels with addresses and quantities for the print distribution, and we separate them all by method of delivery. Then we put each method for each underwriter into a separate bag, and then label each bag with total quantity of books, total number of drops, and the method. Not exactly how you imagined your university degree in action.

"Fuck, I lost count again," he says.

"Want me to do a batch?"

"Nah," he says, tapping through a pile mumbling. "...475, 500, 525, 27, 29, 31... 531." He writes on a bag.

"You know who should be doing this?" he says. "The autistic. We should hire autistic people to break down labels."

I laugh.

"Hahaa, like in Rainman?"

"Exactly. The guy could just throw all the labels on the floor and be like, '356 FedEx! 185 Internationals! 274 Hands!'"

"That's hilarious," I say, laughing.

"And you know what else? I just thought of something!" He holds up his pair of scissors.

I'm smiling at him over our counter waiting for him to continue.

"The goddamn paper jams in the Xerox machine!"

"How's an autistic person gonna help us with that?"

"They can't," he says. "For that, we need…"

I raise my eyebrows as he cuts a staircase though another sheet.

"Wait for it, Laura…"

He points the scissors at me when he's done.

"Midgets."

I crack up. Our industrial-sized copiers have so many drawers and pulls to clear the machine, they run from waist-high down to the floor.

"The autistic and the midgets. That's what we need here," he says, going back to his sheet.

I'm still laughing when the manager walks by.

"Mitch!" my colleague calls out. "We need midgets! And at least one autistic rep!"

Mitch nods and smiles… and keeps walking.

And They Were Never Heard From Again

I went down for a smoke around 9PM. I was in the elevator with a stranger when we got trapped between floors on the way down. We pushed the bell and a guard came and pried the door open a few inches. He crouched from the floor above and his face appeared. In a Jamaican accent he informed us, "It might be some time. Do you want me to send a message to anyone?"

Well, that was kind of him.

He handed us scraps of paper and a pen to write who we wanted him to contact and their extension. We wrote down our bits and handed them up. A few minutes passed and then we saw his feet appear again. Perhaps our rescue was sooner than we thought!

His arm reached in through the slit—a dark blue suit jacket of the building security variety, white cuff peeking out, his fingers outstretched.

And then the voice: "Hey sweetheart, I'm gonna be needing that pen back."

A Few In-House Requests

"Hold on, hold on," the salesman gasps. "You know what we should do?"

We're squeezed into a restaurant booth in London, the three of us laughing over some forgotten joke.

"What?"

"We should prank call Arnie Allen." Arnie Allen's another salesman, back in New York.

We laugh again.

"Stop," Stacie says.

"He's got that group coming in next week, he's so worried about it, I'll call and pretend I'm the client changing it to this weekend."

"Come on," I say, laughing.

"We're doing this," the salesman says, pulling out his phone.

Two bottles of wine in, this is what counts for cheap thrills out of town.

"Quiet," the salesman shushes us as he puts the phone to his ear. "It's ringing."

"Yes, Mr. Allen…," the salesman introduces himself as the client in a slightly tortured Spanish accent. "Our plans have changed, we will be in your offices Saturday, this Saturday… oh yes, definitely all weekend…"

Stacie and I are snickering, holding the stems of our wine glasses as we lean into the table.

"Well, I would say thirty people… oh, yes, a big group… we will need thirty clean proofs…" The salesman holds his finger up to silence us.

"Also, thirty cumulative proofs…" I'm imagining the New York salesman huddled over his notepad taking the instructions.

"And we'll be hungry, so… thirty steaks…" I laugh, this is a salesperson who grubs cigarettes from reps instead of buying his own. "They must be porterhouse steaks, Mr. Allen, please, we must have them… yes, thank you."

Stacie and I are giggling uncontrollably.

"Oh, and also, please, one last request… FIFTY-TWO DANCING GIRLS!!"

At that we all bust out laughing.

Arnie took it like a champ.

Who's Got The Note?

"Who's got the note?" someone calls out toward the end of the shift.

We pass the loose pages of the note around, updating the line by our initials for each of our active jobs working. This is how we facilitate turnover in New York, where there are hundreds of active deals going at once. The note is a simple summary of what's happening on each job, enough to give the Team Leaders an idea how much work's involved so they can make assignments for the next shift. Formal job notes get typed into our system (in all caps because that's the only way our system takes it) for posterity, but the note is handwritten every eight hours—each rep scribbles their contribution to each job onto the template started by dayside—ten jobs to a page, adding new jobs that came alive to the back of the list. When the Team Leaders for the next shift come in, they put new reps' initials next to each job, and off we go for turnover. Our lifeblood, the note is used all shift long to refer to who's working what job and what jobs you're responsible for.

Midnight turnover. Nightside's in a flurry trying to wrap jobs up for turn and third—the lobster shift—is trickling in as the minutes tick closer to midnight. My pages of the note are done and I'm in the midst of typing my real Job Notes into the system.

CONV WKG AT BPX FOR 0600. DLD.

I call up my next job in the system.

OKTP AT BBC FOR 0700. RUN IS 48000. LOCALS 0900, BULK DROP ADP BY NOON, OOT MON. FOLLOW UP.

Sixty people in Customer Service at midnight on a weekday, suited up. Some conference rooms still active, some clients planning to stay all night. There's a whole world being lived here… when most people are tucked in their beds.

"Hey, Shel, is that in-house gonna be here all night or what?" a Team Leader calls out, his pen poised over the note to make the next assignment.

"They're getting close to compsupe, maybe a few hours," she calls back.

A guy from Team B begins his ritual of starting a fresh pot of coffee and I shift my next job bag onto my stack for turnover.

JOB OKTF. SEC ACCEPTANCE OUT. 1-SIDED RUNNING, BLUE TAPE. OG TO CHICAGO TO BE DONE FOR THE MORNING.

Reps, managers, EDGAR personnel. There's gotta be a hundred people on the floor right now once you count IT, Xerox, Shipping, and Composition. And the salesman in the corner, with his feet on the desk and the newspaper across his chest. Even he comes alive when third shift comes in.

REV CONV WKG AT BCL FOR NOON. DLD.

Next.

RUSH AA'S WKG AT BOA FOR SINGAPORE DEL ASAP. NY PROOFS HAND DEL FOR 0900. DLD.

"Is this master up to date?" I hear Tino say to one of my reps. I know the answer, when I hear him slide it directly into the trash.

The phone rings.

"New York Customer Service, this is Laura... Sure, one sec."

I put them on hold.

"Dan, ya got Palo Alto on 8-0," I say, turning back to my keyboard.

JOB IS OKTP FROM BOL. WKG AT BBC, BOOKS FOR FEDEX INTL SAT. COLORWORK OKTP YESTERDAY, SHEETS ON THE FLOOR. DISTRO TO BE DONE.

Most of lobster's here now, milling about, small chatting. There's something beautiful about the third shift guys standing at the counters absentmindedly tying their neckties while reading the pages of the note. Sexy even.

AA'S FROM SKADDEN WKG BPX FOR 0600. OG TO CHARLOTTE, SAN FRAN, AND HOUSTON TO BE DONE.

Next.

2-SIDED FOR ROADSHOW OUT, MAN ON BOARD.

I overhear a nightside rep starting a vent with his counterpart: "And so then I get the turn from dayside and, you know how she is, the turn is like, 'Back when the dinosaurs ruled the earth...'" The lobster rep laughs. "Fuckin' just tell me what I need to know, ya know what I mean?"

ADDL AS FILED OUT FEDEX. BIW.

Next.

CLIENTS DUE IN-HOUSE TMW 10AM TO WORK TOWARD FILING. 15 CLEAN PROOFS RUNNING IN XEROX FOR 0800.

One of the third shift guys is making a round to the printers on our team, refilling the drawers with paper.

HEAVY AA'S ON THE FRENCH VERSION AT BOM FOR 0300. RUSH OG TO PARIS AND LONDON TO BE DONE. NY PROOFS FOR 0900. DLD.

"Hey, Laur, where you guys goin' tonight?"

"Antarctica, I think. You done?"

"An hour maybe, I'll meet you down there."

"Alright."

CLIENTS IN-HOUSE CONF RM 8. EXPECT DUMP & RUN ON LOBSTER FOR AM PROOFS. TRYING TO FILE & PRINT FRIDAY.

The six-man management team is at their counter turning over their key info and priorities. I hear Mitch's distinctive laugh come across the counter.

"LM, you ready to turn?" someone says.

"Yep, one sec," I respond. One more quick note.

NFA. BIW.

"Whatcha got?" I say, standing up from my chair, stacks of job bags behind me.

We're wide awake in this upside-down universe, phones ringing and conference rooms buzzing. And Xeroxes running with pages of the note.

Bates Race

"Bates race by Team A!!" someone shouts from the hallway.

This is the kind of thing we resort to when there's a long slow period in Customer Service. Usually in summertime, when the market's slow. If you hit a slow period, the deals dry up, and suddenly there's not much to do.

We busy ourselves with housekeeping. Go through files of job bags and send lingering deals to Pricing to be invoiced. Clean out cabinets of samples and as-filed books. Windex our desks. Hang out by another team and chat. Maybe the manager will let a few people leave early—we call that a beat out. It's a tough balance keeping Customer Service staffed well enough to support the busy times but lean enough that you don't have to lay anyone off in the slow times.

"Hey, you watch the phones," I tell the most junior member of the team as the rest of us head over to the other side of the building to check out the race.

A crowd had already started gathering. The counter was set up: two reams of paper and two Bates stamping machines, the tool everyone uses to bump up copy for typesetting—a CSR's main task.

Trash talk had started. One of the guys was taking money bets. Tough call, both were seasoned reps.

The challenge was clear. Bump a ream of paper (500 pages) as fast as possible. Whoever finishes first wins. Easy entertainment for a Tuesday night.

There's an art to bumping. The key is syncing the movement in your non-dominant hand to access the corner of the next page as fast as possible, to keep pace with how fast your dominant hand can stamp the machine down to imprint the number.

A Bates stamper is mostly metal—if it's a good one—with a doorknob handle on top that you plunge down to turn the machine's cylinder of digits to the next incremental number.

Coordination, rhythm, speed, and stamina. Bumping 500 pages, stamina is critical.

Half of the Customer Service Department is abandoned as reps gang up around the Team A counters to watch. Some hop up to sit atop counters further out to get a better view.

The guys are prepping. Rolling up their sleeves, shaking their arms out.

"On your mark!" One of the guys from Team A is serving as umpire.

"Get set!" The two reps grip their bumpers, sitting beside their stacks of paper. Position their hands on their stacks.

"Go!"

The sound of two Bates stampers beating in tandem begins.

Dudumdudumdudumdudumdudumdudum

The crowd shouts, people cheer for both sides.

"Woohoo!"

"C'mon!"

"C'mon! You got this!"

"You got a reputation to protect, faster man!"

Dudumdudumdudumdudumdudumdudum

WHOOSHwhomp! Rep #1 slaps his first hundred pages facedown in front of his stack and keeps stamping.

WHOOSHwhomp! Rep #2 is right behind him.

Dudumdudumdudumdudumdudumdudum

"Damn, that's fast," the guy next to me says.

Dudumdudumdudumdudumdudumdudum

I love this place.

This Page Intentionally Left Blank

"These freaking guys…," my colleague said, returning to our bank of desks.

I looked up. "What now?"

"They're not happy with the ILB," he said.

"The ILB??" ILB is an acronym for the "intentionally left blank" page in financial documents. A printed book has to be divisible by four pages, so once the job's imposed, there might be extra pages at the back and ILBs are inserted instead of blank pages. ILBs are also used in between sections to get a new section to start on the proper side of the layout.

"They're in there arguing that the language isn't technically correct because if it says 'This page intentionally left blank' it's not accounting for that fact that those words themselves are on the page."

"Stop."

"I'm not kidding, this is what they're fucking arguing right now," he said, moving some papers around on his desk.

"Tell 'em they can make it whatever they want," I said.

"I did."

BzzzBING!

"Here we go," he said, getting up to go back to his conference room.

He returned with the bookproof swinging by his side.

"Take a look at this shit," he said slapping it down on our median, already flipped to the page.

The clients had indeed marked up the ILB.

"This page intentionally left blank," the standard text read, after which the attorney had marked a caret and added the clarifying disclaimer, "except for this language."

I laughed. "This is hilarious," I said.

"I've gotta re-bookproof the whole fucking job because of this crap," he swept the book away and started punching his keyboard.

"Hilarious," I said again.

"It's not fucking funny. If this happened on your job you'd be freaking out."

"Yeah…," I said, considering. "You're right."

SOP 2000

For Y2K I was in a cabin in Ontario... but alas, that's another story, best told at another time.

I had just finished my first big project at work, which was leading a small team of motivated/involuntarily-enlisted Customer Service Reps in updating 500+ pages of Customer Service Standard Operating Procedures for the Year 2000. It was a tedious business and, as you might imagine, not really a glory project. In fact, the guy who was originally running it left the company. I was a member of the project team and the day after he quit, I went into his boss' office and said, "I'd like to take over the SOP 2000 Project."

And the boss looked up from his papers and said, "Really?"

There wasn't any competition. He gave me the project. And so my project management career was launched!

It was completely extracurricular. I still had my regular job and had to run the project on my own time.

"Why'd you volunteer for that? You don't get any extra money," someone said. But I knew it was the right move. I was already on the project anyway and SOP 2000 was a way to get some profile and prove I could do something besides working deals. It gave me more visibility to management.

Honestly, I credit this project with paving my way to corporate. I learned every freaking nuance of CS procedure and afterwards started getting other small projects and assignments thrown my way.

I wouldn't get fully out of Customer Service for another three years, but it was my first step. My first step off the floor.

Bulldog

After Mitch's promotion, they went through four Production Managers in 18 months. Everyone who accepted the position either left the company or asked to be demoted out of it. Bob Reynolds, who originally hired me when he was the CS Manager, was now the VP of Operations. He asked me to lunch; it'd been a while since we caught up. We sat at a round table in some Italian joint downtown.

"So, whaddaya think I should do about the Production Manager position?" he said, once the conversation wound its way around to work.

"It's a tough position to fill," I said. "Nobody wants it."

"I have to find the right person."

"Good luck," I said. I took a bite of my food. "The job is basically—," I gestured with my fork, "you spend all night on the phone arguing with people."

"I'm sure we have somebody who's good at that," he said.

"Pfft, yeah," I said. Good joke. Our whole business is built around yelling at people from other sites and being yelled at. It's kind of what we do.

"Can you think of anyone who might be good for it?" he said.

"Oh, I don't know," I said, considering. "Second shift is pretty green… And probably no one from days wants to come to nights."

"Probably not," he said.

"The job's a pretty miserable existence. You're responsible for all, supervisor of none. You get all the blame and none of the glory…"

"I think you should take it," he said, cutting me off.

"What?" I laughed. He must be kidding.

"I'm serious," he said, putting down his fork. Shit, he wasn't kidding.

"I'm not qualified," I said, turning my attention back to my plate.

"Whaddaya mean?" Bobby had a way of speaking softly that defied his large presence.

I was happy being a Team Leader on nights. We saw a lot of action, I had a good team and we worked great together. I knew what I was doing.

"I don't know enough about printing. Work and turn, work and tumble? I don't know how the sheets lay out or any of that stuff. Mitch went to RIT. I don't have a printing background," I said.

"I can teach you all that stuff," he said. "But I can't teach anyone else to be a bulldog."

Was he calling me a dog? As a compliment?

"You're my bulldog," he said, removing the doubt.

If Bobby thought being a bulldog was a good thing, well, I guess it was.

"Lemme think about it," I said.

"Fair enough."

We went back to our plates.

I was in the position three weeks later.

PART II

Mikey Y

"There's only two things you need to know about this job."

Mike Yelenovic leaned his elbow on the counter and ticked his pen back and forth as he spoke. His shirt cuffs were rolled up and his tie hung on a diagonal, submitting to gravity. Between us, a small pile of Excel printouts. Rows and rows of what we called The Blotter and The Bullpen. This was how the Production Manager kept track of deals on press, deals about to clear to print, and deals we knew were coming but probably not tonight. Each row one deal, with its specs and key notes squashed next to it in 8-point type—the only place in New York City where the MetLife IPO and the Movado 10-Q appeared as equals.

"One."

I listened attentively. It was my first day as Production Manager on nights. Second shift: 4PM to midnight. More than half the jobs clear to print on nights, after the market closes and the bankers can put the prices in. Mikey Y, as we called him, was my dayshift counterpart. I'd be taking turnover from him every day. He had about 25 years on me experience-wise and had probably already forgotten more than I even knew about financial print.

"You... are the passer... of bad information." He grinned, blond hair falling across his weathered face. This guy was in Vietnam. I knew because there was a tiny black and white photograph taped in his cube of a uniformed 19-year-old Mikey Y with a group of other impossibly young-looking soldiers. He still had the same lanky frame of his younger self.

That was actually the perfect way to describe the constant back and forth between Customer Service and the plant, of which the Production Manager is the conduit. There's got to be a way to fix that, but this is definitely not the time for discussion. My focus right now is to understand whatever Mikey Y turns over to me and to not ask any stupid questions.

I hoped he could see that I got it.

"And, Two..." I wonder if he has prepared this speech or if he is amazingly just spontaneously giving it. We paused for a beat and then Mikey delivered his punchline.

"...Every decision you make will be scrutinized for weeks to come."

He laughed. I laughed. I'm simultaneously impressed and put at ease. Holy shit, I hope I don't fuck this up.

"Okay, let's do this thing," he summed up, signaling the end of my 30-second orientation.

We got into the turnover...

The German Librarian

The desk of the Production Manager is a tight short-walled cubicle packed with a computer, a printer, about a hundred pages of loose work orders in various stages of semi-organized progress, a three-tiered plastic black paper handler that no one uses, a stack of Pantone guides, some loose Epsons of colorwork in progress, a few extra reams of paper, a defunct webcam, a pile of sample books, several ancient messy reference binders, two Customer Service Reps standing at its counter to talk about issues, and a telephone.

The telephone rings. I answer it.

"Seventh ring of hell, how can I help you?" I am the Production Manager and I have caller ID.

"Did you ever get the quantity for that job?" My counterpart at the plant.

"What job we talkin' about?"

"What does the German librarian say?"

"What?"

"What does the German librarian say?"

Okay. Scanning the Excel spreadsheet of jobs expected to clear to print tonight. What does the German librarian say...

Goldman—no.

AIG—no.

Royal Bank of—no.

Monsanto—no.

Republic of—no.

Scanning, scanning—no—no—no.

Got it.

"Reed Elsevier?"

The voice on the other end mimics an old German woman.

"Reeeeeed Elssseviiiier!"

I laugh. I repeat it back to him in the same voice. Laugh again.

"Good one. 30-35K for 7AM."

"Thanks, hon."

"Thanks." Click.

I look up at Rep #1.

"Whatcha got?" I say.

"Reed Elsevier's cleared to print." He hands me the paperwork.

"Hey, what does the German librarian say?"

"Ha ha."

I love my job.

End of Days

I swing out of the Customer Service door and clack past reception on my way to the other side of the department. The papers I'm holding swish back and forth by my side.

"I still can't believe it's your last day," I say to the receptionist without stopping my stride.

"Believe it," she says, barely looking up from her doodles. She's tethered to the desk by her headset, which is carefully arranged around her hairstyle.

I reach the door on the far side of the elevator bank and am about to open it when I notice the band of eight light switches beside it. In a sudden impulse, I flip them all down, leaving reception and its adjoining hallways in pitch black.

She shrieks.

"Gonna miss ya, girl," I say, opening the door and leaving her laughing in the dark trying to detach herself from the desk.

Mr. Baker

It's 7PM on a Thursday when the far door of Customer Service swings open and Mr. Bob Baker strides into the department. He's the President of our company.

Not many from our corporate offices upstairs show their faces in Customer Service, but Mr. Baker knows every rep's name, and more importantly, uses it.

"Good evening, Mr. Pelfrey," he says. Matt Pelfrey's desk is just a few feet from the door.

"Good evening, Mr. Baker."

Mr. Baker walks up the rubber runner into the department proper. Reps are everywhere, walking, hands full of pages, some rushing, some carrying proofs or taking things off printers or putting them onto fax machines.

"Mr. Grant, sharp tie," he says as Darryl Grant walks past.

"Thank you, Mr. Baker. You're looking pretty sharp yourself."

Mr. Baker is wearing a tuxedo, undoubtably on his way to some evening event. He's come down from the floor above via the staircase near reception and is headed to the Shipping Department to pick up his car voucher. He doesn't have to come through the department, and I suspect he knows we know this, and I suspect he knows we know he knows—and that we appreciate it anyway.

"Mr. Mandry, good to see you."

"And you as well, sir."

Mr. Baker makes his way down the wall of cabinets filled with as-filed masters, past the industrial-sized copy machine, and arrives at the row of managers' desks, where he scans the CS Manager's clipboard listing all the accounts in-house tonight.

"How's it going tonight, Mitch?" he says to the manager. They have a chat about the most high-profile deal. A salesman happening by stops to pay his regards.

We're a good company. Over 225 years old, we're the oldest surviving company in New York City, beating out Bank of New York by only a few years around the American Revolution, and we're the oldest public company in the country traded on the New York Stock Exchange.

Mr. Baker has recently implemented the company's first Casual Friday policy. To the chagrin of some, and with firm guidelines that Casual Friday still means business attire: no jeans, collared shirts are a must, no bare shoulders or open-toed shoes, and only for the summer months. Basically it means New York Customer Service Reps don't have to wear jackets or ties on Fridays from Memorial Day to Labor Day.

"Good evening, Ms. Melia," he says to me as he turns his way out of the department. I'm sitting at the Production Manager's desk, the last desk on the row before this half of the department comes to an end.

"Mr. Baker! What's this, first Casual Fridays, now Formal Thursdays?" I jibe.

177

"Ha!" he says, smiling through his gray beard.

"Have a good night, Mr. Baker," I say as he rounds the corner to head to Shipping for his voucher.

"You too, my dear."

I hear his footsteps touch down from our carpet to the other rubber runner that leads out of the department toward Shipping.

"Mr. Hampton, how are you this evening?" I hear him say from the hallway.

"Very well, Mr. Baker." I hear the faint pat of a handshake, as the Team Leader of Team A greets the President.

Mr. Baker's alright in our book.

Cast of Characters

Recently I was reminded of a suave elder member of our Shipping Department. His bowler hat, his money-green shirt and vest.

"The guy made a career outta stitchin' proofs and lookin' good," my colleague reminisced. We share the warm laugh of nostalgia. Our friend has long since passed away, but you'd think we went to band camp the way we "remember when" this place. We're like little old ladies on the stoop.

Stamping his fist down on the heavy metal stitcher to chomp through another 180-page proof, our gentleman would kid the guy beside him, "I do my best work when I'm bangin'."

He had a habit of mispronouncing jobs when he called them from the window.

"Farm-ak-ak—, you know, proofs up!"

Fifteen Customer Service Reps would look up from their desks and at each other.

"What'd he call?"

"Proofs up!" he'd yell.

"Is he calling Pharmacia & Upjohn?"

"Could be."

What a cast of characters we were.

Death by Phone Call

"OK to Bookproof on ImClone," a rep says, dropping the paper-work on my desk and heading on to drop the master with Howard, the bookproof operator.

"Kenny, it's Laura," I say into my phone. "I need two cars. Body uptown on Room 4 round trip and then a heavy to JFK on 36128... Okay, thanks."

Click.

RING.

"Customer Service, this is Laura."

"Hey." Familiar voice.

My other line starts ringing and it bounces to my colleague at the next desk.

"Why are you calling?" I say.

"I wanted to talk to you."

"Laura! The quantity on GiantPharma just went up to 72,000," a rep shouts over from the copy machine.

"Okay," I call back.

"What's there to talk about? We broke up," I say back into the phone, penciling 72,000 next to GiantPharma on my Blotter/Bullpen printout.

"Come on, don't be like that," he says.

"Lau, Lisa at BBC needs you to call her back on the Hong Kong preflight." I nod in my colleague's direction, and stand up at my desk.

"You said... you don't love me," I say quietly.

An uncomfortable pause on the line.

"Laura, I'm sending Chach's tender offer down to Apple," Mitch says walking by.

"Thanks," I say.

"I… I do love you," the voice in the phone says as a rep from Team B approaches my desk.

"It's too late," I say. It's easy to be cold when you're in the zone.

"Come on…"

The rep's at my counter now, holding a board of paste-up and some paperwork, waiting for me to hang up.

"I gotta go," I say into the phone. "Bye."

Click.

"Whatcha got?" I say to the rep.

"Let's talk about the envelopes on Hexbarton," he says, putting his mockups on my counter.

I look down at the hung up phone. Just for a second, but it beats an imprint on my memory. I look up at the rep and lean into my counter.

"Let's," I say.

A Tuesday Morning

September 11, 2001.

   On the street, a woman screamed:

   "Oh my god, it's coming down!"

[This page intentionally left blank.]

Aftermath

In September 2001 I was the Production Manager for a financial printer in downtown Manhattan. I managed the print schedule and delivery priorities for all our accounts in the NYC area.

Returning to work after 9/11 was at once surreal, heartbreaking, demoralizing, and necessary.

The first day back the Shipping Manager came to my desk.

"I need you to see something," he said.

I followed him back to the Shipping Department.

There was an enormous stack of packages in the Shipping Department. They were neatly arranged in a wall about six feet high and at least fifteen feet long. A puzzle configuration of thick and thin envelopes, small and large cartons, all with our company logo on them. Outgoing packages. Hundreds of them.

Our office was below 14th Street, so we'd been closed for days. This must be all the backed up deliveries from when we were closed. The pile was so big. And, shit, they were really behind. We were going to need more messengers to get this out today.

"What is this?" I said.

He leaned toward the pile and touched it.

"Undeliverables for World Trade."

Silence.

The sound of a non-stop Xerox machine in the background.

God. Everything that was supposed to deliver to the World Trade Center that Tuesday morning, practically a week ago now. I looked closer. All these packages. Each one had a label, with a name, a company. A client who didn't exist anymore or who didn't have an office to go back to.

I looked at a few. The law firms, bankers, accountants. Their first names. Did these people get out? WTC1, WTC2, WTC7. The floor numbers. God.

Some packages had notes with instructions for the messenger:

"ASAP!!"

"Must get signature!!"

"Call 212-555-3215 from Lobby and client will come down!"

"DO NOT LEAVE IN MAILROOM!!!!"

How important these things were just a week ago. Everything needed an exclamation point. A fucking intergalactic rush.

So many packages, literally no place to deliver them to.

So many names.

"What should we do with them?" he asked.

I took a breath and let it out.

God.

I looked at the floor. Twisted my pen.

What should we do with them.

What. should. we. do.

I looked at him.

"Dump 'em," I said.

He gave me the eyeball, like to confirm.

"Yeah." Sure now. "Dump 'em. If anyone still wants this stuff they'll call and we'll do it again."

"Okay, you got it."

I jumped in the freight elevator and went for a smoke. Nothing was going to be the same.

Cheese Sandwiches

I sat enraptured as my colleague detailed the odyssey that had taken him from the office on 9/11 through his attempts to get back to his apartment, which culminated in him joining a group of men who had broken into the Burger King across from World Trade in an attempt to procure food for the emergency workers. A makeshift relief effort, they'd set up tables and supplies and made sandwiches all night long for the never-ending stream of hungry responders.

"Oh my god," I said, completely captivated by the tale, and this in a period when every story you heard was more incredible than the last.

He leaned on the counter ledge of my cube, hands clasped, and, in a tone that indescribably captured the sadness, shock, and confusion we were all still feeling, said, "Laura... I must've made a thousand cheese sandwiches."

We looked at each other as I thought about the sheer number of cheese sandwiches we were talking about. The world had gone insane. How were we gonna come back from this?

"So anyway," he said, changing his voice to upbeat, and signaling the topic was closed, "We drinking tonight?"

"Yeah, for sure."

"Great."

He turned and headed back to his desk.

Ground Zero

The days trudged on, but things weren't the same. We kept going out after work, like always, but we were doing it in an effort to make things feel the same and they weren't the same, we weren't the same. We all knew it. We were shadows, and the city a shadow of itself. It was too quiet downtown, something had faded. New York was mourning.

The city that stops wishing people Happy New Year by the afternoon of January 1 couldn't turn the corner on this. We wanted to be on to the next thing but we couldn't move off that day, it was everywhere still. On the street, in the flyers pasted to buildings and fences, in the never-ending stories. In the subway, in the crowd on the platform. In the muted bars and in the sky, tendrils still rising above us, you could taste it and smell it in the air. It was on the sidewalk in every passerby's face. It was in the voice on the phone and in the nervous glances in dead-stopped traffic at the Lincoln Tunnel toll booth. In the sluggish market, in the news. It was the blank space surprising me every day as I turned south onto Washington Street, the shock of empty air in the landscape beyond the Travelers building, beyond Canal, a rote memory taken for granted until now. How long would it take before I wouldn't expect to see them there? It was the eggshell around the yolk of every conversation. September 11 was still everywhere.

"Come up for a last drink."

"I really can't," I said, huddled over my steering wheel.

"Come on, I wanna show you something."

I rolled my eyes.

"It's not like that, I swear. Seriously, five minutes."

When we turned off West Street and around the back of his building... there was a tank. A military tank sitting around the corner from West Street. It was surreal. The guard, officer, soldier (?!) asked us for identification. My colleague explained he lived in the building and the guy let us park.

I'd never been to this apartment before but, suffice to say, when your wife is a banker, your apartment is pretty nice by New York standards. Doorman building. A real doorman too, not just some guy sitting behind a counter in the lobby. Clean, sleek building. Marble. Metal. Mirrors.

We took the elevator up. His apartment was a studio, a strict rectangle, maybe thirty feet deep. Modern kitchen. Wood floors. High ceilings. Place must cost three grand a month, I thought. The far side of the apartment was floor to ceiling windows—a great feature giving the city-dweller maximum light and minimal claustrophobia.

"I've been keeping the blinds closed...," he said.

In less than a second I transfixed our coordinates in my head. Oh, no. He started pulling open the blinds.

A month ago, my colleague and his wife had had a fairly mediocre New York view, its highlight being a possible sliver of

Hudson River sunset visible between buildings if you were standing in the very corner of the apartment and also, as such, happened to not be working during sunset time, which was a category neither my colleague nor his banker wife could claim. Now they had a five-star view of a smoldering hole in the ground. Their apartment looked practically directly down on Ground Zero.

"Oh my god," I said, before I was rendered speechless.

We stood there as the silence beat on. There was nothing to say. Nothing that could be said. There was still activity down there, lights for workers to see at night. All sorts of rubble, spikes and shards of metal sticking up, tiny beings moving about. A red glow, something still burning somewhere. Smoke rising, so much smoke still.

"It's coming in through the vents," he said.

I looked up to the duct near his ceiling.

"Like at work," I replied.

"Yeah."

Americans

In the fall of 2001 I hooked up with a guy from Texas. Just your usual bar hookup; he was in town on business. We were on his balcony in those big white hotel robes watching the 5AM cars come down Lexington Avenue when he quietly, so earnestly, said:

"Tell me about 9/11."

A different time, a different guy, a different mood... even thinking of it now, maybe I should have been offended.

But in that moment, it was a beautiful bit of humanity.

We spent the weekend.

Indenture

I'm on the phone with the plant giving them updates on jobs coming. Job names, account numbers, document types, spec changes. It's a tedious business, this daily ritual of the Production Manager, a manual endeavor ripe with pauses where I wait for him to write down the specs I'm telling him, often repeating myself because he wasn't paying close enough attention or couldn't write fast enough. We do this at least twice a shift. We're halfway through the list when he interrupts me.

"Can you spell that?" he says. Our relationship is not exactly synergistic. Mostly because of its nature, and partly because I miss his predecessor, but more than slightly because I think he's an idiot and he thinks I'm a pain in the ass bitch. Today, we both might be right on that last count.

"Spell what?" I say into the phone.

"Indenture."

"Are you serious?"

"Yes."

I sit back from my Excel printouts. There has to be a line

somewhere. This is the fucking line.

"No," I say.

"What?"

"No, I'm not gonna spell 'indenture' for you. If you don't know how to spell it, you should look it up."

"Laura…"

"Would you like to look it up and call me back or do you wanna finish the list and look it up later?" Once I'm out there I've gotta double down.

He huffs a bit, says I'm not being professional. It's true. It was definitely not the most diplomatic way to handle it on my part, but I've never really been great at choosing my battles. Things build up and then suddenly the fucking word 'indenture' becomes the symbol for everything wrong in the world. Or at least here on nightshift. Because you know what else isn't professional? Being in financial print and not knowing how to spell the word 'indenture.'

"Finish the list," he says.

In robotic tones, we continue.

Tomorrow's another day.

Ya Ever Heard of a Job

Reps over a wall and a Xerox machine:

"Hey, ya ever heard of a job called Jersey Group?"

"Hershey Group?"

"No, Jersey Group."

"Jersey ROOF?"

"Jersey GROUP!"

"What?"

"Jesus. Ga-ROUP! Jersey GROUP."

"Oh, Jersey Group?"

"YES!"

"Nah, never heard of it."

Suspicious Package

"New York Customer Service, this is Laura," I answered the phone.

"You manager?"

"This is Laura Melia. I'm the Production Manager."

"This Security. We have suspicious package. We holding for you, come get." Our security guards were not completely assimilated to the English language, but they did their jobs.

"Whaddaya mean, suspicious? What is it?"

"Come get," he directed.

"Okay," I hung up and walked the fifty or so feet around to the elevator banks' Security desk. He had an envelope. It didn't look all that suspicious except that it didn't have a name or address on it. It was a 9 x 12 plain white envelope that had our company name handwritten on the front, which, come to think of it, was a little suspicious. It was the thickness of one or two printed books.

"Where'd you get this?" I asked.

"Downstairs bring up."

"Someone dropped it in the lobby, and the lobby guy brought it up to you?"

"Yes." Odd. Messengers came up to our floor all the time, especially with client packages. In fact, it would be extremely odd for a messenger to even have a package that just had a company name with no address or person named on it.

"Alright," I said. I took the package to my desk.

Back in my cube, the girl next door looked over the wall.

"Does this package look suspicious?" I asked her. There'd been a lot in the news of anthrax and suspicious packages. Security was on alert.

"Yes," she said.

"Looks like it's probably printed samples in here," I said, feeling the contents. "It feels like one printed book. It's definitely a printed book."

"Don't open it," she said. "It's not even addressed. That's really weird."

"What are we supposed to do, just leave it here unopened forever?" I searched my drawer for a razor blade. "I won't rip it, I'll just slice the end open." I placed the package flat on my desk.

"Be careful," she said, hanging over the wall of the cube now.

I sliced the end of the envelope open. Leaned my head down toward the desk so I could look inside without having to pick it up again.

"BE CAREFUL!" she said as I lifted the edge.

"Oh man."

"What?" she said.

"It's another envelope."

"Oh my god! Please stop now."

"It's okay." I slid the second envelope out of the first. Looked carefully into the first. "Nothing's in here," I said.

The second envelope definitely contained a printed book, you could see the outline of the book along the edges, it was wedged in there tight. I pressed the envelope against the cover to read the name of the deal.

"Well, that's weird."

"What?" she said.

"It's a book but it's not one of our jobs." Perplexing, really. I started slicing the second envelope open.

"Laura, please be careful!!"

I pulled the book out. Definitely a book. Definitely not one of our jobs. Who sent this? Why?

"What is this?" I said to her. "Who sends a random book?"

"Are you sure it's not for Team C?" She sat back down in her seat. Team C worked all intercompany deals, jobs for salespeople of other US offices.

"I don't think so…" I was flipping through it. "Oh my god," I said, dropping the book open on my desk.

"WHAT?" she said, from the other side of the wall.

"Look."

She leaned over.

About halfway through the book, there was an envelope taped to one of the pages. A white #10 envelope, just taped there in the middle of a printed sample.

"Oh my god, Laura, that is DEFINITELY SUSPICIOUS!"

I poked the outside of the envelope.

"There's something in it."

"DON'T OPEN IT! It could be anthrax!"

"Hold on, it's okay."

"PLEASE don't open it."

I sliced the pieces of tape holding the envelope in place, releasing it from the page.

"I can't watch!" she said.

I felt the envelope. Bent it.

"Uh oh," I said.

"What? Laura?"

"Well, it's not anthrax," I said as I opened the flap.

"What is it?" she peeked her head over.

I opened the envelope toward her. Inside was a wad of cash.

"Uh oh," she agreed.

I put the package back together. Brought it back to the Security desk, where the shop steward of the elevator operator's union was interrogating the guard.

He came toward me as soon as I turned the corner. "You got my package?" he said. He was fuming.

I held it out and he grabbed it.

"You opened it?"

"They called me 'cause it was suspicious."

"Fuck that, suspicious, don't fuckin' open my packages." He purposely bumped into me and started stomping away.

"Tell your guy to put'cha name on it next time," I called after him.

"Fuck you."

"Yeah, you too."

I stole a glance at the security guard—his back motionless, his head professionally directed at the elevator bank—and headed back to my desk.

In Our Lifetimes

"You see, you have to remember at that time the only women who worked here were secretaries and receptionists... So, I'd like to say I was welcomed... but I wasn't."

—Veteran on what it was like to be the first saleswoman at Bowne of New York

Negotiation

"Where you guys at?" Murphy shouts over the bar noise in the background.

"Tribeca Tavern," I shout into my phone.

"We're at Walker's."

"Well, we're at Tribeca Tavern."

"Come down to Walker's," he says, laughing.

"Come to Tribeca Tavern!" I laugh back as my colleague hands me a beer.

"Jesus Christ, woman." he says. "Fine."

Freebie

"What the hell is this?" Matt says, poking the empty french fry sleeve laying on our counter for the midnight turnover.

"You know that freebie job for Team A, the one with all the logos?" I say.

He puts his hands on his hips and I see the shadow of the young man he was twenty years ago in the Military Academy.

"Yeah."

Some call him the Gentle Giant, which he is—kind, good-hearted, completely client-centric, a towering figure who does things the right way. He doesn't cut corners. I sleep well turning the Production desk over to him, never worrying that he'll forget a key detail or that he'll miss something I would have caught. But oy, when he gets mad… I recognize the place it comes from in myself, and we share that unspoken camaraderie of the darkness. The darkness that comes not from evil, but from a fight with yourself.

But tonight's nothing to get mad about. It's just a freebie for Team A. An annoying pain in the ass freebie with a dozen logos on it. And one empty french fry sleeve.

"That's what they sent in for the McDonalds match."

He lets out a guffaw. "You've gotta be kidding. They want us to pull the PMS from this?"

"Yep." It's been done, it's not the best way, but we can match whatever.

"Unbelievable," he says, shifting his heavy frame.

"You didn't notice the best part?" I say, nodding him a smirk.

"What's that?"

"It's dirty!!"

He takes a closer look.

"Oh my god! He ate the fucking fries out of it!!"

We have a laugh. We do the turnover.

RIP my friend, you were one of the good ones.

War in Busy Season

President Bush declared war against Iraq tonight.

I watched his speech with Mitch on the TV in the darkened client lounge at our office on Hudson Street. It was after 10PM and it felt very somber. But then again, it was barely a year and a half since 9/11; we were still checking packages for anthrax, deleting World Trade Center clients from the Rolodex, breathing in garbage through our A/C vents.

Plus, it was busy season.

We watched the broadcast silently.

"Wow," I said when it ended.

"Yeah," he said.

And then we went back to work.

Summer 2003

"What's goin' on with you, girl?" Debby says to me as we converge in a hallway, heading back to Customer Service. "You look different these days, new man?"

"Yeah…," I say. Debby and I started the same day; we've known each other for years. She's so much more girl than I am though—blonde, blue-eyed, bubbly personality. If I had half her fashion sense, damn, if I could just tie scarves the way she does… "I guess, it's only been a few months…"

"TELL ALL!" she says as we clack our way down the hallway.

"There's nothing to tell, it's crazy, I guess I'm just… Happy." Shit, is this what happy feels like? I think so! This is honestly the first time I've felt it. Wow, that's what I am: happy. I don't want to speak it but I think this guy's the one. He's got to be.

"Yeah!" she says. You can't help but smile when she's like this, and so I do. "Good for you," she says. "I'm happy *for* you."

"Thanks, chickie," I say, as we split off to head to our separate desks.

"Rock on, woman!" she calls back over her shoulder.

Some years prior, when I'd gone through a bad break up, Debby sent me an email. A pep talk, a great one actually, that ended with a "PS: send this back to me the next time I need it."

Thanks, Deb, for making me notice that summer of happiness.

Costco Membership

"So, today I finally go to Costco to get a membership," I say to the Assistant Manager in the cube beside me.

"Yeah...," he says.

"Did you know they take a picture for the card?"

"Do they?"

"Yeah. So of course I go there thinking it's an in and out thing, I'm practically still in sweatpants, my hair is in a bun..."

He sits back from his terminal.

"When I realize they have to take a picture, I'm freaking out. I mean, who knows how long I'm gonna have this photo on my card. I look like a mess!"

He appears to be losing interest in my story.

"So, whatever, they take the picture, they make the card," I reach into my bag and slide my new Costco membership card out of my wallet. "And take a look what it looks like." I hand him the card over the short wall of our cube.

You'd expect a photo ID to, I don't know, be a close up of the person's face, right? My new Costco picture looks like it's taken from 20 feet away and my head makes up two fuzzy black and white centimeters in the upper right corner of the square. The hair I was so concerned about is indistinguishable from the background.

My colleague takes the card, squints at it over his keyboard, and giggles.

I am vindicated.

Blackout

I was still at my desk in downtown Manhattan an hour into the Blackout of 2003 when it dawned on me how easy it is for us to do nothing.

We didn't know it was just a blackout. Still jittery from 9/11, we tried not to panic as we called our other offices on the rapidly draining backup phone power trying to find out what was going on. When my colleague yelled out, "Cleveland doesn't have power!!" that's when we started to worry.

My friend appeared and huddled over my desk. "This is like World Trade," she said, "They just waited for someone to tell them to leave."

In that moment I realized nothing had changed. After everything, we were still fucking sitting there.

We grabbed some waters and made for the stairwell.

Outtakes

"I'm wearing your sister's red panties."
—Note handed to a colleague by her male co-worker while she was talking to a client... she put it in her pocket, forgot about it, and got it back from her dry cleaner a week later

"I don't care if she's on her deathbed. I want my copy of the fucking document."
—A client's response to being left off the distribution list while attending to his dying relative in North Dakota, pre-email

"I like to watch the boats."
—Law firm partner, dressed in full military camouflage, on why he would like his group moved to a conference room facing the water

"Who'd you talk to? Someone on my crack-squad of savvy, motivated personnel?"
—On interdepartmental communication

"Sir, I don't know what your workplace is like, but at my office we have a phone, a fax machine, and a computer. My setup does not include a crystal ball."

—Rep to a client who sent us something and thought we got it but never informed us (we didn't get it) and kept giving us crap that we should have known it was coming

"Well, you'd better get used to it, 'cause I'm probably gonna have to flush again."

—A salesman's retort after we expressed disgust that he was flushing his toilet while we were giving him an account update over the phone

"You're right. When we found out, we sat around and looked at each other. And then we just laughed and laughed and laughed."

—Rep to a client who felt we weren't taking his missed filing as seriously as he was

"I don't care if they're using voodoo and finger paints... as long as they get it done."

—One reflection on whether Customer Service needs to know the details about Composition's internal processes

"Fuck off, I'm busy."

—I'm told I once said this to someone from Pricing when they approached me with a question ten minutes before the SEC's filing deadline. Actually, she claims these are the first words I ever spoke to her. Sorry, Linda!

"Yeah, you, go find us a paper stretcher, three halftone dots, and 50 feet of redline."

—Imaginary things you ask a new rep to locate in the heat of battle

"Got any colored pencils?"

—Working group member at 10PM the night they were clearing to print when they realized their company did not have a logo

EXHIBITS

Flashback, Interview

"So, tell me about this job you have, the one at the answering service," Bob Reynolds said, placing my resume down. He was a big man with a buzz cut, sitting across the tiny table in one of the cramped interview rooms of Fordham's career center at Rose Hill. He was a Fordham grad, like I was about to be, and the Customer Service Manager at a New York City financial printer called Bowne & Co.

I didn't know anything about financial printing, or printing for that matter, or about publishing in general, or finance in general for that matter. I was an English major. In preparing for the interview, I'd read the key summaries of Bowne's last two Annual Reports, which were on file at Fordham's career center library, and that hadn't cleared things up at all. There was no internet to get more information. All I knew was they were a company hiring, they were accepting applicants who were English majors, and I needed a job. I had a vague notion of what customer service was, I mean, I was a telephone operator, I dealt with customers I suppose. I had experience helping customers. Financial Print Customer Service helped customers, I guess. I could do that.

"I'm an emergency telephone operator," I began my prepared response. "I answer the phones for doctors' offices and heating companies when they're out of the office. I take messages and decide which calls are true emergencies and get in touch with the doctor if necessary. I work the evening shift so it's pretty busy since all the offices are closed. We take calls from patients, hospitals, other doctors…"

"When it's busy, what's it like there?"

I smiled.

"Oh, the phones are ringing off the hook. It's kind of crazy actually. The calls are coming non-stop, all the operators are talking at once, papers are flying in the air." He cracked a grin.

I was getting a little off-script, but what the hell, I felt encouraged. "I answer literally hundreds of calls a night. And it's kind of a physical job. We have this console we put all the messages into, and that's also where we keep the info on where the doctor can be reached—it's kind of hard to describe, it's like a multi-level cylindrical wheel that spins around and everybody's turning the different levels to get to the account they're answering."

I was way off-script now. "Things move really fast, you have to be able to remember numbers and account details, special things about each doctor."

What the hell was I even saying?

"And, you know, a lot of people who call are frustrated or upset or sick, it's not like just answering the phone and taking a message. Patients yell at you. The doctors can be pretty demanding. And then the hospitals, that's a whole other story…" Jesus, I was screwing this up, babbling on.

But he was smiling. Why? I didn't know. Does he think I'm an idiot? Probably. I sound like an idiot.

I stopped myself from continuing, and told myself to practice the interview art of sitting there and knowing when to shut up. I sat there uncomfortably, suddenly extremely conscious of the oversized suit jacket I had borrowed from my mother.

He was looking at his papers, still smiling.

"I'm sorry, I got a little carried away there," I said.

He shook his head and looked at me. Seconds ticked by excruciatingly while I waited for him to say something.

"I think you might like it in our Customer Service Department," he finally said. "Would you mind also speaking to my colleague next door?"

"Of course not. I'd love to," I stood up. "Thank you, Mr. Reynolds. It was good to meet you." I held out my hand for a shake.

"You too, Ms…" He looked down at my resume. "Melia. Good to meet you." He opened the door and directed me down the hall.

I had no idea what just happened.

In the next room I sat across from a woman named Terri Hansen, who informed me she was the Team Leader of the newest Customer Service Team at Bowne, the International Team. This meant nothing to me.

She took a look at my resume.

"You live in Ridgeland?"

"Yes," I said.

"Oh wow, you're on Park Street? That's right around the corner from me!"

"Really? What street are you on?"

She told me.

"You're right! Wow, that's crazy," I said. She really did live right around the corner. We chatted a little about the neighborhood. She told me how she was a new mom.

"Alright," she said, "We'd better get down to business, I'm supposed to be interviewing you."

"Yes, okay." I waited for the first question.

"So, tell me…" She smiled. "Do you do any babysitting?"

Autumn in New York

It's 2011 and my friend and I are retired. Or willfully unemployed; it depends on your perspective. We've both left the industry, for now anyhow, and we spend autumn in New York wandering the city at midday—traipsing through Central Park or up and down the city blocks aimlessly—and eating. Bowls of ramen in Hell's Kitchen. Tapas in Chelsea. An afternoon of antipasto on Amsterdam. A quick bite at Shake Shack. We're on an eat and a walk, in deep chats about life and meaning.

Our chats are not so different than the ones we had years ago, when we were in Customer Service together, and we'd squeeze into a tiny table at Ino's after our shift at one o'clock in the morning. A bottle of wine, a plate of olives, a bowl of roasted garlic. Bread.

We're older now, wiser maybe, more tired for sure.

"Is Ino's still around?" I wonder.

There are no answers. Still. But at least now we're glad we don't have to work tomorrow.

We're meandering down from a cake boutique on the Upper

East Side and pause to window-shop a collection of incredibly crazy high heel shoes.

"Look at those," she says.

"God, how do you even walk in those?" I say.

A random lady passing by gives us a proper New York moment by interjecting without stopping her stride: "Honey, ya don't walk. Ya take a car service."

We're in giggles on the sidewalk forever.

Hey, Howard

Years ago, I worked with a petite bespectacled unassuming gentleman named Howard. Our cubes were next to each other at the printer's on the floor of Customer Service; we were the final stop before a job went on press. I was the Production Manager and Howard made the bookproofs, which were the last version the client reviewed to clear a job to print.

Only a short wall separated our desks and we had a lot of laughs, ordered a lot of dinners, and pushed a lot of deals through the shop. We'd get on a call every day with Lee at the plant and banter it up, Howard pounding away on his calculator doing the form breakdowns for whatever jobs were coming that night.

I was in my 20s and Howie was in his 40s, but we made a good team. Howard's defining characteristic at work was that he would get increasingly anxious the more work we had to do and the more CS would tell him things were a rush, which was basically... daily.

"I mean it, Howard, SUPER RUSH!" they would tease him.

"Howard! What are you doing? I need this done in like 20 minutes, I already told the client 20 minutes max!" (standard turnaround was two hours).

One time a rep told him, "Howie, get a move on. My tie cost more than you pull down in a year."

That one was a little over the line.

"Stop bothering Howard," I'd say.

You could tell how stressed Howard was by the way he answered his phone.

"Helloooo?"—easy day.

"Yes, this is Howard"—not so much.

When things got really bad, he would just pick up the phone and stutter, "Yes, yes, okay, okay," and then he'd hang up and go for a smoke, breezing by an approaching salesperson. Sometimes I'd tell CS to pile his work on my desk and I'd hand it off to him piecemeal. Things worked better that way.

Maybe Howie wasn't built for stress, but his work product was 100%. He cared about the client. He'd complain all night long but when it came down to it, he'd get it done. He'd hustle, forever scooting around the counter to where his printers were and back again, brushing his hair out of his face. He made the operation better, creating his own little systems and processes for his job. Maybe in another life he'd have been a graphic designer or a film critic or, who knows, something more creatively fulfilling than bookproofing twenty lots of mutual fund prospectuses or 10-K after 10-K after Notice & Proxy Statement during busy season. But he wasn't those things.

"I'm just the bookproofer," he'd say.

I don't even know what he did before Bowne. But he saved our asses a hundred times finding whacked out folios, making up time we needed for the print run, or doing the shit work of cleaning up some fax-of-a-fax-of-a-fax crap before a job went on press.

In the tense months after 9/11, every time I got a package Howie would wheel up to the wall and tilt his head in.

"Is it... anthrax??" he'd say in a breathy voice as I peeled open the envelope.

"It's the Goldman samples, Howie."

"Suspicious, verrrry suspicious," he'd smile. These were the small things that kept us on the border of sane.

One day we were sitting there and Howard said, "You know, there are people who have jobs... and there are people who have lives..." He paused before cackling, "And none of those people work here!"

He had one of those dorky laughs that was an inhaling laugh, like if you're breathing in while you're laughing.

He introduced me to sushi and a whole array of foreign take-out foods available in New York City, mostly by force.

"Just order ANYTHING, Howard! I'm fucking starving!"

Whatever he ordered was always good. Howard had really great judgment about food.

How he loved to travel. He'd take his whole four weeks vacation in one drop, flying off to another trip of a lifetime every year. Once he went to China and I asked him to bring me back something.

"Ooo like what?" he said.

"I don't know, how about a set of chopsticks?"

"What kind? There are a lot of different styles..."

"Any kind, I don't care."

"Laura, there are like a million to pick from..." He began listing different materials and types.

"Howie, get whatever's cheap, they'll be special 'cause they're from China. Pretend you're going to Midtown and buying a fork."

He brought me back a gorgeous set of black chopsticks with intricate floral designs on the handles. When I asked how much I owed him he said, "Don't worry about it, it was like buying a fork."

Thanks, Howard.

Every time he left for vacation, he'd taunt me, "Laura, you'd better get used to doing bookproofs, because I might not come back."

"Howard, you're coming back and we're gonna have a whole pile of Cravath legal briefs the day you return."

"Ohhh noooo!" he would say, faux-shaking. Those things were like 600 pages of camera-ready-copy. Howard hated scanning.

One year he went to Thailand and, true to his perpetual threat, he didn't come back. His brother said he died in a surfing accident but I was pretty sure Howie faked his own death. Days passed and managers put up the notice about his services. I didn't go. I regret it but at the time I just couldn't. Howard couldn't really be gone. I liked believing Howard was somewhere in Indonesia in a hammock laughing about us being stuck doing his bookproofs. Weeks passed and the guys from other shifts sat in Howard's chair to fill in.

Slowly his desk became less Howard, things with his handwriting disappeared, and, as always, life went on. Jobs cleared to print and bookproofs got done and I gave Lee the updates and learned how to do the form breakdowns and I ordered my own dinner.

I'm not sure exactly why I stole the calculator from his desk as a memento. I kept it in my drawer for a while, absurdly thinking if he came back he'd want to have it. Finally I took it home. I use it all the time. It reminds me to remember him.

And, hey, Howard... I missed you.

Happy Anniversary 2015

I give my husband an anniversary gift and part of the wrapping has a square of burlap. We worked in the same industry, for competitors; that's how we met.

"Can I just tell you seeing this burlap is giving me flashbacks of a crazy deal I worked?" he says.

"Really."

"Yeah, it was a mining company that decided it would be a good idea to attach little sacks of burlap with a piece of coal inside them to the prospectus."

"WHAT?" I say.

"Yeah, we were getting ready for the OK to Print and the sales coordinator's like, 'You're not gonna believe this but we need to find a company that can stamp onto burlap…'"

"Ohmygod."

"Yeah."

"So, what, you bought little burlap bags, had a vendor stamp the logo onto them and then what, the company delivered a bin of coal? That's hilarious," I say.

"Yeah. And I'm not talking about a bin of coal where each piece was like three-quarters-of-an-inch-size either. They sent a bin of coal where we had to go at it with, like, little pick axes and stuff."

"Ohmygod," I laugh. "And then what? Shipping put the pieces in the bags?"

"Shipping? Laura, please, TEMPS. Temps put the coal in the bags…"

"Hahaaa I'm trying to imagine this. I mean your hands get dirty, even if the temps are wearing gloves, they have one hand holding the bag, one hand picking the coal, now one hand's dirty… how do they tie the bags? Wasn't everything getting dirty?"

"Well, it wasn't that dirty but let's just say a few of the books had to be dusted off," he says.

Hahaaahaa.

"And, what, the bags had a little drawstring?"

"Oh my god, THE STRING, that was a whole 'nother problem. We couldn't find a string that looked good, could knot, and was strong enough to hold onto the book. We tried a few strings, the company didn't like the way they looked. We ended up having to order a hemp string or something."

HA!

"And then you tied it around the book?" I ask.

"We hole-punched the upper left corner by the spine and tied it there."

"Jesus. How'd you even ship it? You can't put that in a regular envelope… ohmygod you had to get boxes?"

"SPECIAL ORDER BOXES, Laura."

"This is hysterical. I have to go write this down."

"This is what happens when you have the wrong people in the

room," he says, fingering the square of burlap. "The run was only 500 or something, but still. So painful."

"What's crazy is like, from the shareholder's perspective, you get your prospectus delivered and it has a piece of coal attached to it? Who wants that?"

"Yeah, well, the company went under about three years later."

Circle of Life

His window to retirement in sight now, every day he looks a little more gleeful. Over the last twenty years I've been in his office— in its many iterations—more times than I can count, sometimes yelling about something, sometimes being yelled at, lots of times just figuring stuff out. Whatever the case, jobs and clients and changes keep coming and Frankie is in it, always insisting, "We'll get it done."

I'll confess: plenty of times I didn't believe him.

Love him, hate him, I've never met another in this industry who has the client's interest at heart like he does. These last few months I've taken notice in meetings as he rolls off operational considerations with the second nature you only get by being in a business for forty years. It really is beautiful.

Then there's his experience and the personality he brings with it. You know somebody? He knows them. Got a whackadoo requirement on your account? Seen it. Capacity question dealing with completely intangible factors? He made that formula up back in the '90s. And it works! Let's talk about big corporate changes—mergers, takeovers, mass hiring, mass layoffs, relocate your office, grow a business, bring on new vendors, make your department spin with life-shifting technology... You wanna turn the whole thing inside out or maybe bring it back home again? Done it all—probably more than once.

But the best part is he knows the history. More than that: he holds the history, he tells it. He's a caretaker of it. The history is so important.

And so as the days tick toward that big circle on his calendar, in the afternoons he takes off his jacket and tie. He's been packing up his million mementos from a lifetime spent in print, and I'm feeling so sentimental.

There's still things to do.

He says we'll get it done.

I believe him.

And I'm looking for a few more times I can get him to say, "Good job, kid."

xxx

GLOSSARY

10-K, 8-K, other number/letter references — See Form Types

AA's — Author's alterations, i.e., edits to the document

Bannerline — A set of information and codes at the top of a page in a proof that verifies its identity, version, and location in the document

Bates stamper — The hand-held machine used to stamp identifying marks, typically an account number and cornermark sequence, onto client markup

BBC — Bowne Business Communications; the Secaucus, New Jersey, manufacturing plant

Beat out — Leaving work early due to slow activity in the department; a manager gives beat outs, reps get beat outs

BIW — Bag in Wheel; the "wheel" was the circular filing system at Bowne of New York in decades past; by my time the actual wheel was gone, but the terminology remained; any filing cabinet that held job bags was referred to as "The Wheel"

Blotter/Bullpen — The Excel spreadsheet used by the Production Manager to keep track of jobs on press, jobs about to clear to print, and jobs to come

Body uptown — "Body" is the shorthand used to order a car to carry a passenger, typically a client; used in conjunction with the general direction the car needs to take the passenger (e.g., "body uptown" or "body downtown," as differentiated from "package uptown" or "package downtown")

Bookproof — Final version the client reviews to clear a job to print; it's an imposed mock up that resembles the printed copy, showing blanks, ILBs, and color breaks

BPX — Bowne of Phoenix, the largest typesetting site

Breakout — An additional smaller conference room used by an in-house group

Bump, Bump up — The act of Bates stamping a job

Bust a page — When a client makes an edit to a page after it's already cleared to proof, file, or print

Busy season — Roughly the first quarter of the calendar year when an influx of work arrives as companies prepare their Annual Reports and Notice & Proxy Statements

C2 — The act of starting a new round of blacklining in a typeset job; "C" or "current" proofs show marks from the last time a new round is started

COB — Close of Business (loosely, 5PM)

Color break — Identifying marks to show what colors different elements of a job will print in; the point or line at which one color gives way to another color

Colorwork — Parts of the job printing in 4-color process, in financial print typically only the covers; can also refer to spot colors, like a logo or red herring

Composition Platform — All the typesetting sites across the network working together as a whole unit, flexing jobs between them as capacity demands

Compsupe — The composition function of repaginating a document; the term is shorthand for the "Composition Supervisor" screen in the typesetting system where the action takes place

Conversion/Convert new — Transforming a client's native (Word, Excel) files to the typesetting system

Cornermark — A stamp or number in the lower right corner of a page, used as an identifier as the page moves through the typesetting shop

Correspondence — The official tag for the letter to the SEC that accompanies a submission being filed

The Counter — open-air pass-throughs on either side of the Customer Service Department; wide counters clients can walk up to for immediate access to a Customer Service Representative

CPOs — Changed Pages Only; the pages of a document affected by client edits

CS — Customer Service

Days, Dayside — First shift in Customer Service; reps working 8AM to 4PM

Delivery List, Distribution List, aka Greensheet — A formal list created by Customer Service that details who is to receive material, what material they are to receive, when they should receive it, their contact information, and what method (messenger, fax, FedEx, international courier, man on board, etc.) should be used to deliver it; gets its slang from the green paper it's printed on to distinguish it from the rest of the papers with a job

Diskfax — A machine used to transfer files from one office to another (pre-email)

Distro — Shorthand for a Delivery List or Distribution List

DLD — Delivery List Done; the Delivery List instructions are complete, not that the materials have gone out

Dump and run — The act of an in-house group working in our conference room for hours without handing in any markup, and then dropping a ton of pages at once for us to work when they leave; the "dump" typically occurs between 11PM and 3AM for morning proof distribution

EDGAR — An acronym for Electronic Data Gathering Analysis and Retrieval; the SEC's electronic system for receiving, accepting, and processing corporate filings

Exhibits — Required supporting documents that accompany an SEC filing

Fax game — Like an in-house, but clients are off-site; the clients fax markup, we make the edits and fax back changed pages on an immediate-turnaround basis; continues back and forth like this for multiple rounds

Filing package — A compilation of pieces for a formal SEC submission, involving a letter to the SEC, multiple clean and marked tape-bound copies of the filing and its exhibits, with executed pages for original signatures and a copy sequentially stamped; paper filings were hand-delivered to the SEC and have since been phased out for electronic filings

Finals — The final books that are printed and delivered to shareholders, such as a prospectus or offering memorandum; see also "Preliminary"

Forms, Form breakdowns — Organizing the way the sections of pages (forms) of a job will be divided for printing on press

Form types — The submission types required to be filed with the SEC for various corporate activity events; the SEC has hundreds of form types defined, for example, an IPO is filed under a Form S-1, an Annual Report under Form 10-K, and current report activity under a Form 8-K

Greensheet — See "Delivery List"

ILB — Intentionally Left Blank; a standard page inserted into financial documents to force pagination to lay correctly or to substitute blank pages

In-house — Clients working on their document in real-time in our offices

Job — One deal

Job bag — The physical container of a job's paperwork, proofs, and records; it's an oak tag expanding file sleeve

Job notes — Customer Service's written narrative that records the activity of a deal

Job number — The account number that identifies the deal

Lobster, Lobster shift — Third shift in Customer Service; midnight to 8AM

Man on board — Putting a person on an airplane with a package to deliver; used when standard delivery means cannot achieve the required delivery time

Markup — Client edits, written by hand on the document

Master — A copy of the document that is the most up to date version of the document

NFA — An acronym for No Further Action; it means you haven't executed any activity on the deal on your shift

Nights, Nightside — Second shift in Customer Service; 4PM to midnight

The Note — Handwritten summaries of what's happening on each deal, used to facilitate turnover; not the same as "job notes"

OG — An acronym for Output Graphics, our method of transmitting proofs to other cities for delivery (there was no method of emailing or creating PDFs at the time; CS would "OG" jobs to offices in other cities and reps in those cities would pull the files down, print them out, copy them, and deliver them per instructions)

OKTF — OK to File

OKTP — OK to Print

OOT — Out of Town

Pantone, PMS — Pantone Matching System® (acronym PMS); a standardized color matching system devised by the Pantone company to ensure accuracy of color, an industry standard

Patching a master — The act of manually replacing out of date pages in a master with new ones

PN — Page Number; a serial number in the bannerline of a typeset page indicating the page's order in the document

POD — Proof of Delivery; the name of the person who accepted delivery of a package and the precise time of delivery

Preflight — An analysis of a file for print-readiness

Prelim, Preliminary — A draft of the book that prints once the company has initially filed with the SEC; it contains most of the information a prospective shareholder would review about the company, however does not contain the price or number of shares offered, and is still subject to amendment and is not finalized; because the SEC requires its disclaimer language be printed in red ink, it is also informally called a "Red Herring" or "Red"

Proof — Any draft form of a document output from our systems; typically sized 8.5 x 14" to accommodate bannerlines and allow space for client markup

Prospectus — A required legal document filed with the SEC that details an investment offering to the public

Red Herring, Reds — A preliminary book, its name taken from the red disclaimer language printed on the front cover that tells a shareholder the registration is not yet effective

Redweld® — A type of heavy-duty expanding file folder commonly used by attorneys, typically dark red in color

Rev Conv, Rev Con — Abbreviation for reverse conversion, the act of changing a document on our typesetting system back to a word processing application, usually done at the end of a deal so clients can commit internal edits before the next one or repurpose the contents for other uses

Roadshow — When an issuer travels around the country to present a securities offering to potential investors, fund managers, and analysts; meant to generate interest in the transaction, some version of the printed books is needed for the roadshow

Runners — People whose sole job is bringing things from one department or person to another

S-3 — Form S-3, see Form Types; a common security registration form that includes a prospectus

SEC — Securities and Exchange Commission; the agency of the US federal government that regulates the nation's securities industry and stock exchanges

Submission — A filing with the SEC in electronic format

Traffic — The department responsible for coordinating the movement of people and packages to and from the office

Turn, Turnover — The passing of jobs and information from one shift to the next

Turn and burn — The act of a Customer Service Rep feverishly turning over their jobs to the next shift and then rapidly exiting the building before all hell can break loose

The Window — a counter pass-through between Customer Service and the Shipping, Traffic, or Xerox Department; "calling a proof from the window" means someone is yelling to CS that a proof is ready

Working group — The array of clients involved in a specific transaction, including representatives from the company or issuer, banks, attorneys and accountants for all parties, and perhaps designers and other ancillary parties

Work order — A formal document issued by Customer Service to record activity on a job; an instruction to other departments to execute specific tasks on a job; every work order has a corresponding Delivery List to indicate which clients should receive the product of the work order

NO TYPESETTERS WERE HARMED IN THE
MAKING OF THIS BOOK

ABOUT THE AUTHOR

Laura Melia Kelly was born in Brooklyn, New York, and has lived in the New York City area all her life. She attended Fordham University at Rose Hill and graduated with a BA in English. She's been writing since childhood. After her time in Bowne of New York Customer Service she worked for Bowne & Co., managing corporate projects affecting Customer Service offices globally. She retired at 36, took a hiatus, and now makes cameo appearances in the print industry as a consultant. She still talks too loud and too fast, but is working on the talking back part.

Body Uptown is her first novel.

Website: www.laurameliakelly.com
Facebook: www.facebook.com/laura.meliakelly
LinkedIn: www.linkedin.com/in/lauramkelly

Sign up for news on future publications at:
www.gatefoldpress.com